Twitter Means Business

How microblogging can help or hurt your company

By
Julio Ojeda-Zapata

HappyAbout.info

20660 Stevens Creek Blvd., Suite 210
Cupertino, CA 95014

First Printing: November 14, 2008
Paperback ISBN: 1-60005-118-9 (978-1-60005-118-0)
Place of Publication: Silicon Valley, California, USA
Paperback Library of Congress Number: 2008941050

eBook ISBN: 1-60005-119-7 (978-1-60005-119-7)

Trademarks

Warning and Disclaimer

Praise for this book

"Julio's book on Twitter is the first business-minded book about the topic that I feel comfortable recommending to companies wondering why they should consider the tool for their organization. I've found a resource that I will share effusively."
Chris Brogan (@chrisbrogan), social-media authority at chrisbrogan.com

"Julio brings us the first handbook for companies that want to properly understand, learn from and engage with the uniquely powerful social-media phenomenon that is Twitter. His crisp, clear writing style and thorough research make 'Twitter Means Business' an accessible point of entry for anyone looking to learn more on the topic."
Laura Fitton (@Pistachio), Principal and Founder, Pistachio Consulting

"Twitter just might be the best place on the planet—or the universe—to grow a new audience. 'Twitter Means Business' gives you a jump-start on the best practices and social-networking etiquette you need for success."
Veronica McGregor (@VeronicaMcG), creator of the acclaimed @MarsPhoenix and other space-mission Twitter feeds

"Think microblogging is all about announcing what you had for lunch? Think again. In 'Twitter Means Business,' Julio offers compelling case studies that demonstrate the power of engaging customers in this emerging social-networking platform—140 characters at a time."
Bryan Person (@BryanPerson), Social Media Breakfast founder and LiveWorld social-media evangelist

"Millions of people gather around the new water cooler known as the internet and talk about products, services and brands. Only now what they say is permanent, archived and searchable. The bad and the good never go away. In this book, Julio gives excellent advice to businesses on how to participate in one of the major water coolers on the web—Twitter—and come away with not just more good than bad said about them, but new legions of loyal brand fans."
Jason Falls (@JasonFalls), Doe-Anderson social-media director and SocialMediaExplorer.com author

Author

- Julio Ojeda-Zapata
  http://twitter.com/jojeda and http://twitin.biz

Publisher

- Mitchell Levy
  http://happyabout.info

Edit and Content Layout

- Teclarity
  http://teclarity.com

Cover Design

- Cate Calson
  http://calsongraphics.com

Dedication

To Jeaneth and Leonel, whose love and patience made this possible.

Acknowledgments

A few thank-yous are in order. Thanks to Mitchell Levy, founder of Happy About, who learned about a Twitter-related newspaper article I was researching and suggested I be a bit more ambitious (good call). Thanks to Cate Calson, who did such a terrific job on the front cover. Thanks to the talented Liza "Nitrozac" Schmalcel, who is responsible for my awesome cartoon-style likeness on the back cover (please drop by the Geek Culture site operated by Nitro and her partner Bruce "Snaggy" Evans at geekculture.com). Thanks to my editors at the St. Paul Pioneer Press, who were so patient when I was juggling book work and day-job duties, and tending to crankiness. Many thanks to Albert Maruggi from the social-media sphere and Jennifer Leggio from my own tech-journalism realm for their great bookends. Gracias to Mom and Dad, for cheering on their firstborn's big project so loudly. Thanks, especially, to my wife and son for their love and support; this is for you!

A Message from Happy About®

Thank you for your purchase of this Happy About book. It is available online at http://happyabout.info/twitter/tweet2success.php or at other online and physical bookstores.

- Please contact us for quantity discounts at sales@happyabout.info
- If you want to be informed by email of upcoming Happy About® books, please email bookupdate@happyabout.info

Happy About is interested in you if you are an author who would like to submit a non-fiction book proposal or a corporation that would like to have a book written for you. Please contact us by email editorial@happyabout.info or phone (1-408-257-3000).

Other Happy About books available include:

- I'm on Facebook—Now What???:
  http://happyabout.info/facebook.php
- I'm On LinkedIn—Now What???:
  http://happyabout.info/linkedinhelp.php
- Internet Your Way to a New Job:
  http://happyabout.info/InternetYourWaytoaNewJob.php
- Happy About Online Networking:
  http://happyabout.info/onlinenetworking.php
- Tales From The Networking Community:
  http://happyabout.info/networking-community.php
- Happy About Customer Service:
  http://happyabout.info/customerservice.php
- The Emergence of The Relationship Economy:
  http://happyabout.info/RelationshipEconomy.php
- 42 Rules of Marketing:
  http://happyabout.info/42rules/marketing.php
- Marketing Campaign Development:
  http://happyabout.info/marketingcampaigndevelopment.php
- Blitz the Ladder:
  http://happyabout.info/blitz.php
- Marketing Thought:
  http://happyabout.info/MarketingThought.php
- Expert Product Management:
  http://happyabout.info/expertproductmanagement.php
- They Made It!:
  http://happyabout.info/theymadeit.php
- Collaboration 2.0:
  http://happyabout.info/collaboration2.0.php

Contents

Foreword by Jennifer Leggio

Twitter changed my professional life.

If you had asked me about it a year ago, I would have had a snarky reply, like "What a silly name!" or, "Who needs to know what I'm doing all the time? or, "You mean, like 'twitterpated'?"

Most internet users still scoff at the name when they hear it, even with exposure in the New York Times and on CNN, and mentions by top political candidates and television shows.

Scoff I once did. Lucky for me, I happened to participate in a social-media webinar that encouraged its participants to sign up for the microblogging service. That turned out to be one of the best professional things I ever did.

I first used Twitter as a kind of public instant-messaging system—a faux pas that many newbies commit. I would post thoughts such as, "Going on a date tonight!" or "I really want some pizza," or "Seriously, is anyone listening?"

Shockingly, people were. I improved my game. I began discussing issues I saw in the communications industry, and began dialogues about computer-network security and enterprise-technology issues that are close to my heart. (Yes, you can do this in 140-character snippets.)

I peppered all this professional-speak with hockey chatter, improvisational comedy-isms and other personal-yet-not-too-personal thoughts that make me who I am. I realized that people would not only talk to me because of my professional prowess but because they could relate to me as a person.

That is the essence of social media, no?

My social-media standing up to this point was nearly imperceptible, even though I was an avid blog reader and used Facebook, among other social-networking tools. When I would comment on blog posts, I'd rarely get a response.

Now, after months of talking to my favorite bloggers via unidirectional commentary, they were finally writing back—in 140 characters or less, on Twitter.

I found that Twitter is more than a communication tool—it is an engagement tool. Unlike blogs that emphasize a single author's thoughts and allows reader comments as a bit of an afterthought, Twitter fosters true two-way conversations. I was suddenly having many of these.

Before long, my Twitter chatter had led to more business- and technology-related lunches and dinners than I ever thought possible. It helped me pull together an online community of like-minded network-security types.

I developed a kind of personal "brand" courtesy of Twitter while enhancing the brand of my employer, a leading network-security company. Twitter gave me a new way to listen to my company's customers and its partners, and to support our sales and support teams.

It was my deepening understanding of this tool, and the grounding it gave me in social media, that eventually led to my role as a technology blogger and commentator. I write about all things social media—and particularly how they relate to business endeavors.

While Twitter is easy to use, its simplicity can be deceptive. Using it in business can be tricky, and takes much more than sitting in front of a computer and banging out random 140-character sentiments. Exploiting Twitter the way Comcast, Zappos and JetBlue have requires a grasp of its nuances and the many ways it can be used in a business context.

That's one of the reasons why "Twitter Means Business" is such an important read for entrepreneurs, CEOs, communications professionals and anyone else in business who wants to learn how to engage customers or their own employees via the Twitterverse.

The stampede of businesses into the Twitterverse is proof that Twitter isn't a flash in the pan. Even with aggressive consumer-microblogging competitors, along with a new class of companies trying to create corporate-grade microblogging services, Twitter endures.

It's the microblogging service that started it all. It's a story you must understand, even if you eventually migrate to other microblogging services. After reading this book, you will get it. Then you can say that Twitter changed your life too.

Jennifer Leggio has worked in the strategic-communications industry for 15 years, most recently at a top network-security firm. She writes about business social-media trends on her prominent ZDNet "Feeds" blog, a part of CNET. She founded and co-runs a social-networking community for the network-security industry. She's @mediaphyter on Twitter.

Foreword

1 Why Twitter Means Business

Comcast was annoyed with me. Specifically, a senior Comcast executive in the southwestern United States, far from my Minnesota home base, was irked with something I said on an internet service called Twitter.

He told me so. To be more exact, Scott Westerman "tweeted" this. That is how millions now interact on the internet. Twitter, a kind of "social networking" service, allows them to publish their thoughts in the form of brief text snippets or "tweets." A tweet cannot exceed 140 characters. Once tweets are placed online, anyone can see them and respond.

Among Twitter-using pals who "follow" each other on the service, this is hardly unusual. Twitter has become a popular way of socializing via PCs and phone text messaging. But the fact that a faraway Comcast executive whom I didn't know happened to pick my tweet out of the millions published every day and take the time to respond, was remarkable.

That's what this book is about. Twitter means business. That is, a service initially meant for informal communication between individuals has recently become the darling of businesses, large and small. Such firms are finding the "Twitterverse" a fine place to keep an eye on their brands, and what is said about them. They are creating Twitter accounts and making friends with other users.

This is how Westerman and I connected. He, like a number of other Comcast employees, was monitoring the Twitterverse for mentions of his firm. He didn't answer all such tweets (key staffers at Comcast's Philadelphia headquarters are paid to do that), but took it upon himself to respond selectively. Westerman found my tweet[1] using a keyword search, mere minutes after I had posted it one April afternoon, and fired off his mildly indignant reply.[2]

I was so surprised and flattered to hear from such a high-level Comcast executive that I later interviewed him for this book (see Chapter Two). Comcast is one of several dozen Twitter-hip companies profiled in these pages. Some are giant corporations; others are small family-run companies. All have found Twitter to be invaluable as a business tool.

If you're reading this book, you're likely with a company that has heard about Twitter and wants to learn more. Or maybe you're part of a public-relations (PR) or online-marketing agency that advises companies and thinks Twitter might be worth a look—for you, your clients, or both. This book also looks at PR agencies that have become Twitter believers.

Twitter: From Blather to Business

Twitter might seem like the last place on the internet any self-respecting company would want to do business. It can be a trivial and childish realm, filled with blather about bodily functions, pet excrement and what users had for breakfast, lunch or dinner. I plead guilty to this, tweeting about such inanities as my beloved burritos. I even came up with a mock observance, Burrito Avatar Friday, with a different burrito as my user picture or "avatar" every week (my followers have come to expect this morsel, and I can't disappoint them).

---

1 twitter.com/jojeda/statuses/799893624
2 twitter.com/wscottw3/statuses/799909787

Chapter 1: Why Twitter Means Business

Twitter seems to encourage such triviality with the question it places above its text-input window: "What are you doing?" (To which I reply, "Eating a yummy burrito, of course.")

The Twitter format alone might give a respectable company pause; how on Earth can it utter anything of significance in chunks of 140 characters or less? And who would care?

Yet, for all its perceived and real inanity, Twitter has recently seen an influx of companies that have set up accounts and begun using the service for everything from sales and customer service to internal communication and hiring. Turns out the 140-character limit is a boon; Twitter is easy compared to other ways of communicating online, like blogging. (Twitter is sometimes called "microblogging" because tweets are like teensy blog posts.) Just tweet something; this takes all of a minute. Companies are now doing so with gusto.

Twitter is hardly the only place for such companies to create a presence online, beyond their own sites. The web is in the throes of a "social media" revolution that emphasizes two-way communication, a huge change from the old days when companies only had to post information online and let others digest it. Today, they're engaging their customers in web discussion forums, on blogs, and on social-networking services like Facebook.

Twitter still lacks Facebook-level popularity. If you mention Twitter to college students, you will often get blank stares. While consumers increasingly depend on social media to share customer-service stories and find buying help, Twitter isn't one of their top picks. Thirty-nine percent of candidates recently surveyed by the Society for New Communications Research said Twitter and similar services (like Pownce) had "no value" for consumer research.[3]

Yet, still the companies come. The reason: Twitter is on fire. Its users are a remarkably vocal, energetic crowd. More and more businesses want this energy to rub off on them, and seek to generate some fireworks of their own as they discover their inner tweeters.

---

3 sncr.org/2008/04/22/new-study-indicates-consumers-use-social-media-t o-share-customer-care-experiences-and-research-compa- nies%E2%80%99-customer-service-reputations

How Twitter Can Help Your Company

Twitter is your window into a world where your company is likely a topic of discussion. Think about that for a second. Hundreds, thousands—or even millions—are talking about you. What they say—good or bad—is priceless information, regardless of how you act on it. Some companies use Twitter passively, absorbing what is said in the Twitterverse and factoring it into their decision making. Others are active, using Twitter to offer information and to engage their clients and prospects.

Bottom line: Paying attention to Twitter should be a top priority.

How Twitter Can Hurt Your Company

The worst thing you can do with Twitter is to ignore it. That's when real damage can be done to your bottom line, especially if your customers are somehow unhappy about you, and saying so in the Twitterverse. Tweeting is so quick and easy that Twitter users tend to vent about their frustrations. So what if they are frustrated about you? They'll say so; bet on it. And if their tweets contain misinformation about your company, you could get into trouble, as false rumors about you spread at the speed of the internet.

Bottom line: Pay attention to Twitter.

Companies that neglect their brands on Twitter will sometimes see their company names or products hijacked by people not related to their organizations. In one recent, notorious case, an account associated with the Exxon Mobile business giant was revealed to be the handiwork of a person who didn't work for that corporation.[4] The Twitterverse is replete with corporate brands that are being hijacked, or simply being neglected by their owners.[5]

---

4 chron.com/disp/story.mpl/side/5920513.html
5 facereviews.com/2008/08/12/33-brands-that-suck-on-twitter

So Who Is On Twitter, Anyway?

Twitter, though hardly the leading social-networking service on the web, has grown at a rapid clip.

In fact, Twitter was the fastest-growing social network as of September, logging 343-percent growth over the previous year with a leap from about 533,000 users to about 2.4 million users, Nielsen Online announced in mid-October.[6] As of April 2008, traffic to the Twitter site had grown eight-fold over the previous year, according to another internet-tracking firm, Hitwise.[7]

Twitter was the most popular microblogging service as of last summer, with traffic that far surpassed that on rival services like Pownce and Jaiku, according to Hitwise. As of mid-summer, Twitter traffic was twelve times greater than that of Plurk, and about 24 times higher than that of FriendFeed, two services often cited as Twitter alternatives.[8]

According to site-analytics service Compete, Twitter saw more than 2.5 million unique visitors as of August 2008, a 443 percent increase over the previous year.[9]

Friendfeed did little better than 500,000 unique visitors between August 2007 and August 2008, with flattening traffic towards the end of summer, according to Compete.[10] Jaiku and Pownce had a fraction of this, with Jaiku doing the best at just over 160,000 unique visitors.[11] And while upstart Plurk saw a surge in interest at the beginning of 2008 and peaked at nearly 350,000 unique visitors around June, traffic declined sharply after that.[12]

---

6 netratings.com/pr/pr_081022.pdf
7 weblogs.hitwise.com/us-heather-hopkins
/2008/04/twitter_gaining_momentum_but_s_1.html
8 weblogs.hitwise.com/heather-dougherty
/2008/07/twitter_growth_continues_despi_1.html
9 siteanalytics.compete.com/twitter.com/?metric=uv
10 siteanalytics.compete.com/friendfeed.com/?metric=uv
11 siteanalytics.compete.com/jaiku.com+pownce.com/?metric=uv
12 siteanalytics.compete.com/Plurk.com/?metric=uv

Many Twitter-traffic calculations don't even account for use on mobile phones, which is common. This means Twitter could be vastly more popular than statistics show.

Twitter doesn't release its own user or traffic figures, but co-founder Biz Stone told me in August that the service had "grown six times over in the last 10 months. It has strong growth."

To put Twitter in perspective, though, Hitwise in April ranked it 439th among websites it calls "social networks and forums," and 4,309th among all websites. Such figures meant it hadn't achieved mainstream popularity, as other social-networking sites like MySpace, Facebook and YouTube arguably have.

This hardly makes Twitter inconsequential. The raw number of users tells only part of the story; it's also key to note who these people are. Those on Twitter tend to be "the thought leaders, early adopters and influencers" on the internet, said Mike Keliher of St. Paul, Minnesota, based Provident Partners, a public relations and social media consulting agency, which watches Twitter closely.

Such people include online celebrities like Leo Laporte, the tech-podcast mogul and radio personality, and Robert Scoble, the irrepressible video blogger. They also include social-media experts like Chris Brogan of CrossTech Media and Jeremiah Owyang of Forrester Research. Also on the list: Barack Obama, who overtook web entrepreneur Kevin Rose as Twitter's most-followed user as of mid-August, and TV personality Stephen Colbert. Obama had about 105,000 followers (an unprecedented figure) on the eve of the presidential election.

Even millions of lesser-known Twitterers tend to run in tech-hip and web-savvy circles. Twitter attained critical mass, after all, at the super-geeky South by Southwest Interactive Conference in Austin, Texas, early last year,[13] attended by thousands of social media and "new media" types, and the service remained an attendee favorite at this year's SXSWi.

---

13 blog.wired.com/monkeybites/2007/03/twitter_is_ruli.html

What such people have to say about your company, therefore, carries more weight than their modest numbers might initially suggest. So overlook or dismiss them at your peril. Twitter-savvy companies do the opposite: They pay attention to them, and engage them.

The View From Twitter HQ

Some web-savvy companies are not only wooing Twitter users, but Twitter itself. For a number of firms, a visit to Twitter's San Francisco headquarters is a rite of passage. The Nevada-based online retailer, Zappos, made a courtesy call earlier this year (you'll read a lot more about the legendary Zappos later in this book).

So did Mighty Leaf Tea Co., based just across the Golden Gate Bridge in Marin County, California. Mighty Leaf staffers arrived at Twitter HQ earlier this year with massive amounts of gourmet tea (Twitter staffers like it) and gave the Twitter troops a presentation about how the tea vendor had begun to harness the service in its business. Its Twitter account had gone online at about the same time another special-ty-foodstuff supplier, the famed Whole Foods of Austin, Texas, started its Twitter account. (More on Whole Foods later.)

For Bliss Dake, Mighty Leaf's Vice President of E-commerce and Op-erations, that was an exciting time. He was mulling how to make tea and technology intersect, and figured that Twitter was the key. He en-visioned tapping a ready-made audience of web sophisticates who know classy tea bags (the Mighty Leaf kind is handcrafted and biode-gradable) when they see them. He'd start tweeting about tea, get answers from fans, and really mix it up.

Twitter is "an amazing way to connect with people instantaneously," Dake later told me in an interview. "Lots of our customers are out there—what better way to reach them?"

Twitter's Stone hears a lot of that lately, and said, "We're excited. We think it is great."

Twitter's creators had mulled such ambitious business use when they created the service in 2006. But Twitter was then a side project within a podcasting company dubbed Odeo, and "We kind of scaled it back. It was too broad a vision. We scaled it back to just people saying what they were doing."

Stone and two Odeo colleagues, Evan Williams and Jack Dorsey, spun off Twitter in the spring of 2007 (Williams is now Chief Executive) and have since endured a bumpy ride, as their brainchild has suffered all manner of service outages. Twitter has been so unreliable at times that its "fail whale," the cartoon that is displayed in browsers when the service is inaccessible, has become an unofficial, ironic mascot emblazoned on t-shirts and mugs[14] (and at least one tattoo[15]).

Stone attributes the service's problems in part to its rampant growth, and staffers' initial inability to "scale the service." It has been playing a continual game of catch-up as it has become popular, he said, and it needs to "focus on getting ahead of those growing pains, getting ahead of the wave and not being in a crisis situation day to day."

It appeared to be making headway by late this year, logging only 41 minutes of so-called "downtime" in September and 54 minutes in August, compared to more than 11 hours in July, more than 12 hours in June and more than 21 hours in May, according to Web-tracking service Pingdom.[16]

Amid these problems, Twitter has made it easy for third parties to create Twitter-related sites, services or software to augment the experience. This has spawned a vast ecosystem of Twitter enhancements that have helped cement its popularity amid competition from other microblogging services.

This third-party support for the Twitter technology has been "a big surprise," Stone said, "a very big and pleasant surprise."

---

14 zazzle.com/failwhale
15 inquisitr.com/2600/epic-fail-whale-tattoo
16 pingdom.com/reports/vb1395a6sww3/check_overview/
?name=twitter.com%2Fhome

Stone also has been surprised by the degree to which companies have lately been willing to get on Twitter, despite its problems. The business world has been quicker to embrace the service than it has with other internet technologies such as blogging in years past, he said. He's amazed with how the Whole Foods grocery chain, JetBlue Airways and Comcast, among others, have learned to use Twitter in a variety of ways.

Such corporate use had become so important to Twitter by late this year that the service was mulling whether to begin charging companies for their business-related tweeting. This was part of increasing pressure Twitter faced by the autumn to begin making money, something that hadn't been a major priority for the service since its inception.

Companies on Twitter "are getting a ton of value" from the service, Stone told me in October, "so it makes sense to consider a revenue model."

This book documents dozens of corporate-Twitter case studies, and more are out there in the Twitterverse. As this book went to press, the migration of companies onto Twitter continued unabated. Big newcomers included Best Buy, Home Depot, Starbucks, Sprint Nextel and Popeye's Chicken & Biscuits.

So how can your company use Twitter? Oh, the possibilities...

Listening

One of the first and best ways to use Twitter is in stealth mode. You don't have to tweet a thing, just watch and listen. What are your customers saying about your company or your products, positive or (heaven forbid) negative? It's a snap to find out via keyword queries on specialized search engines such as Twitter Search, owned by Twitter, and Tweet Scan.

This turns Twitter into an early-warning system (like a canary in a coal mine) for spotting negative buzz and heading it off before it does real damage to your bottom line. Ignoring negative online commentary about your company could really hurt you. Just ask the computer maker, Dell, which once overlooked a top blogger's complaints about its laptops and soon was associated with the buzzphrase "Dell Hell." Dell now listens closely on Twitter.

Companies that have Twitter monitoring down to a science include the Blip.tv internet-video company, which distributes daily reports among staffers about what was said about the company on Twitter. Blip.tv has been adept at spotting and addressing user discontent before it festers. At Salesforce, a provider of business-management services, a key staffer uses web search tools to find and analyze all that is being said online about his employer, including on Twitter.

Twitter users are a vocal, influential crowd, so you need to know all they say about you. It's so easy; you have no excuse. You can do it in-house, or hire a search specialist like Radian6 or Techrigy to do it for you.

Speaking

Eager to speak out? Twitter is a great place for companies to do so. It's easy; just tweet in 140 characters or less. And what you say can have a major impact. Got hot deals? Dell has made big money by advertising its deep discounts on computer hardware via Twitter.

Want to spread the word about your cool new product? Evernote, maker of internet software, has drawn an unusually large and loyal following on Twitter, where it keeps its customers apprised of updates to its note-taking applications for PCs, Macs and iPhones.

Companies that have boosted their e-visibility include the Holiday World and Splashin' Safari entertainment complex in Santa Claus, Indiana; candy maker Mars Snacks, in the guise of a sultry "Ms. Green" M&M; consumer product giant Unilever, in the guise of the popular Klondike Bear associated with ice cream bars; and Sonos, maker of audio equipment.

Such efforts will have varying degrees of success. Firms that are crassly commercial may experience a Twitter backlash or just be ignored by the Twitterverse. A light touch with this, however, can pay off in a major way—Just ask Evernote and its thousands of followers.

Engaging

Companies aren't using Twitter to its full potential if they are only broadcasting and not interacting with their customers. Twitter is all about conversations—among individuals, and also between businesses and their clientele, who appreciate seeing some semblance of humanity in the companies that sell them airplane tickets, cable internet or tax advice.

Monolithic companies like Comcast and Dell admit they once paid little attention to what their customers said about them online, much less engaged that clientele in conversation. They paid dearly for this. Comcast's low rankings in customer-service surveys are richly deserved, as the company's own Vice President of Customer Service recently admitted to me.

Now Comcast is on Twitter, finding people who talk about the company and responding to their questions and concerns. So is the multifaceted H&R Block tax-service company, which is trying to change the perception (one customer at a time) that it is solely a strip-mall entity. So is JetBlue, which has a way of startling Twitter-using travelers who get its tweets out of the blue. So is Whole Foods, the popular organic- and natural-food grocer, which has displayed a knack for replicating its loyal offline following in a Twitter-based form.

Evolving!

For firms embracing Twitter heart and soul, the service can have a transformative effect.

Look no further than Zappos, the Nevada-based online retailer, which has made a crusade out of Twitter. Its CEO is a prolific tweeter, and Zappos urges its employees to use the service on the company's behalf as well as their own. This turns them into company champions.

The benefits of using Twitter can be internal as well as external; at Zappos, it has fostered communication among its workers and become a promising tool for recruiting new talent. Even in darker times, when the company is laying off workers, these find strength in their Twitter unity. Zappos and Twitter are virtually synonymous.

A Boston-area Twitter star called Laura Fitton—known on the service as "Pistachio"—is more proof of Twitter's transformative powers. The business consultant was laboring in relative obscurity in early 2007 amid a difficult move to Boston—just in time to have her second child. She felt very isolated at that time.

"I had no contacts," she told me in a phone interview. "I was a homebound mom of two, not knowing anybody, not having the luxury to join the Chamber of Commerce."

"Twitter opened up so many doorways," said Fitton, who was initially skeptical of it, but promptly harnessed it to make friends, develop a loyal following (of more than 7,300, at last count) and become a "global presence," in the words of social-media authority Shel Israel:[17]

"Laura has been a communications professional for over 15 years. Yet, if you have heard of her, I'm willing to bet it has been in the last year or so. And I'll double the bet that however you have heard of her, there is a direct line on the social graph that goes directly to Twitter where she is known simply as 'Pistachio.'"

Fitton's Pistachio Consulting firm once focused on presentation coaching for businesses. As this book was being finished, she had re-launched her consultancy to focus on helping businesses understand and effectively harness online "microsharing," including Twitter.[18]

"I've seen what has happened to my own career just using Twitter," Fitton told me in our chat earlier this year. It has "tremendous power."

The Rest Of This Book

Here is what to expect in the rest of "Twitter Means Business."

---

17 redcouch.typepad.com/weblog/2008/04/twittering-her.html
18 pistachioconsulting.com

Chapter Two: In "Five Companies on Twitter," I offer five detailed case studies. The companies profiled in this chapter—Dell, Comcast, JetBlue, Whole Foods and Zappos—have led the way in corporate Twitter use. They use the service in different ways, which shows the flexibility and versatility of this still-new and novel medium.

Chapter Three: In "More Companies on Twitter," I offer a dozen quick-hit case studies focused on the likes of H&R Block, Mars Snacks, casino giant MGM MIRAGE, music-gear maker Sonos and internet-software publisher Evernote. I look at Twitter use in the media industry, as well.

Chapter Four: In "Twitter and Public Relations," I delve into public-relations agencies that use Twitter. As the PR industry has embraced Twitter en masse, it is persuading its clients to give it a look. Firms such as the Graco baby-product maker are now using Twitter, thanks to advice from public-relations advisers.

Chapter Five: In "The Twitter Veterans Weigh In," I share the wisdom of experienced users. I recently hosted a Twitter-based conversation among members of Social Media Breakfast Twin Cities, a group composed of people with deep Twitter and social-media experience. They had plenty to say about how companies are using Twitter.

Chapter Six: In "Twitter Tips, Tricks and Tools," I walk you through the service basics and then dig deeper, showing you how to bend the service to your will. An ecosystem of services and software is available to Twitter users, and I point you to the best stuff. I note Twitter competitors, and show how to juggle multiple services.

Epilogue: My employer and I became a case study for this book as I was writing it. I am on staff at the Minnesota-based St. Paul Pioneer Press, and I have touted it informally on Twitter. In September, my editors formalized this by having me tweet on the newspaper's behalf during the Republican National Convention in St. Paul. It was quite an adventure.

A Note About Twitter Style

When identifying Twitter users, I'll use their full names as well as their Twitter handles or usernames. In keeping with Twitter tradition, I'll precede such usernames with the "@" symbol. I'm @jojeda for personal tweets, @PiPress at the Pioneer Press and @twitinbiz for book-related use.

Throughout the rest of this book, I will quote some Twitter content verbatim. Let's look at one of my tweets, to understand Twitter syntax:

jojeda: Happy Burrito Avatar Friday, everyone.

When one Twitter user makes a reference to another user, this is usually done by typing that person's username preceded by the "@" symbol somewhere within the body of the tweet. When someone names me in a tweet, for instance, they will compose that posting something like this:

jongordon: Ladies and gentlemen, it's Burrito Avatar Friday. See @jojeda

When one Twitter user addresses another directly in a public tweet, the username of the recipient goes at the beginning of that tweet:

jongordon: @jojeda I expect a NEW burrito avatar every Friday. Don't even think about recycling old burrito images.

The tweet recipient can then reply:

jojeda: @jongordon I will do my best to accommodate—though I should note that last Friday's very colorful avatar has wormed its way into my heart.

2 Five Companies on Twitter

Amid a stampede of companies into the Twitter-verse, a handful are Twitter trendsetters.

Comcast, the long-troubled cable provider of internet, telephone and television services, arguably has the most mainstream buzz. JetBlue Airways and Dell have been touted as Twitter stars, too. Whole Foods, a relative newcomer, has shown it can develop a Twitter following in little time, and nurture it with humor and creativity.

The Zappos e-tailer is this book's Twitter poster child. No company has embraced the service more fully and enthusiastically; other companies can learn much from this one.

Comcast

When Shawn King of Danbury, Conn., was having problems with his Comcast internet connection early last May, he griped about it on Twitter:

ShawnKing: Seriously looking into FiOS. Comcast sucks here.

King, who co-hosts the popular online technology talk show "Your Mac Life," had been trying to upload sound files to internet storage but was stymied by slow transfer speeds. This made him so furious he was ready to abandon his cable-based Comcast service and switch to Verizon's Fiber Optic Service (or FiOS).

Within 15 minutes, King got an unexpected Twitter reply:

comcastcares: @ShawnKing Can I help change your impression? Or fix whatever the problem may be?

King promptly tweeted back in what would become a lengthy online exchange:

ShawnKing: @comcastcares Sure! Who are you and how can you help? The issue is speed/throttling of my account.

King had stumbled on one of the finest, most famous examples of a U.S. company doing customer service on Twitter. Frank Eliason, a staffer in the company's Philadelphia-area headquarters, joined Twitter as @comcastcares in early April, and by October had logged more than 16,000 tweets as he reached out to users with technical issues or axes to grind.

Many such axes have been ground. Comcast is a company with an image problem largely based on years of less-than-stellar customer service. Its customer satisfaction ratings fell to an all-time low this year, ranking at the bottom for cable and satellite television firms, according to the University of Michigan's American Customer Satisfaction Index.[19]

"I think that's fair," Rick Germano, Senior Vice President of Customer Operations, told me of his company's abysmal ratings in this and other surveys. "We're not trying to deny it."

This is the company that spawned Comcast Must Die, a now-infamous website created by writer and broadcaster Bob Garfield. The site immortalized the Comcast technician who dozed off in a home while on a

---

19 theacsi.org/images/stories/images/news/0508Q1.pdf

Chapter 2: Five Companies on Twitter

service call, and the famed elderly "Hammer Lady" who wreaked havoc in a Comcast office after being kept waiting for home service for six days.

Garfield's site also allowed Comcast customers to air complaints; hundreds who did so received follow-up calls from the company to resolve their technical problems. But they now have an alternate place to do that: Twitter. In one now-famous case, tech blogger Michael Arrington of TechCrunch, the group-edited blog about technology startups, lost his cool after 36 hours without internet access and vented on Twitter; Eliason answered, and Arrington's access was soon restored.[20]

King said he was disbelieving when Eliason reached out to him. "Yeah, bite me, dude," the famously-frank Macintosh-computer authority recalled thinking. "I had no faith that Comcast did, in fact, care, or that it was paying attention to Twitter. It's so easy to fake a Twitter account. You can say you're Steve Jobs."

King said Eliason turned him around. The Comcast staffer "seemed very helpful, seemed to actually want to help. It did seem that Comcast cared. I looked at his Twitter feed and saw that he didn't get into arguments with folks who are baiting him. He seemed to be a fairly nice tech-support guy."

Eliason, a customer-service manager at Comcast's headquarters in Philadelphia, said he began monitoring Comcast mentions on the internet early this year—focusing mostly on blogs at first, and adding Twitter a few months later. "I try to have a conversation," with those mentioning Comcast, he told me, "to get involved every chance I get." Most react to his unexpected overtures in a positive way, he said, but a few have called it "creepy."

Indeed, a keyword search for the words "Comcast" and "creepy" can be eye-opening.[21]

---

20 techcrunch.com/2008/04/06/comcast-twit-ter-and-the-chicken-trust-me-i-have-a-point
21 search.twitter.com/search?q=comcast+creepy

Eliason gets up early, hits Twitter "first thing" and disposes of some of the customer emails that also make up a major part of his job. Then, after dropping off his kids at day care, he digs deeper into Twitter via search engines (including Tweet Scan and the former Summize, now built into Twitter) to see what the Twitterverse is saying about Comcast.

Eliason can do a lot from his desk at the office, and even from home on his work laptop. Upon activating his virtual private network (VPN) connection to his workplace, he has access to diagnostic tools that allow him to troubleshoot any Comcast customer's connection and modem from afar. So whenever someone on Twitter howls about internet problems, he's able to do something about this, or to "escalate" it so technicians in the area can assist.

Eliason tries to be more than a corporate drone on Twitter. He does not shy from talking about his personal life:

comcastcares: I am home with my 6 month old today because she is sick. I ask our 2 year old if she wants to stay with Dad. She responds NO! GO TO SCHOOL.

Arrington, along with a guest appearance on the popular This Week in Tech podcast with Leo Laporte, helped put Eliason on the map. By the time he was featured on ABC News and in the New York Times in late July, he was arguably the best-known Twitter user in corporate America, with a respectable following of about 2,500. By October, he had more than 4,000 followers.

But Eliason isn't Comcast's Twitter pioneer. That would be Scott Westerman, a Tucson-based Company Vice President who oversees a southwest portion of the country. This is his official job description, anyway. The "unabashed geek" was an early Twitter user. He has served as a sort of national ambassador, scanning the blogosphere and the Twitterverse for Comcast buzz on his laptop while in meetings, and firing off responses if appropriate.

It was Westerman who turned Eliason on to Twitter; the two Comcasters have sometimes worked as an informal customer-care team, in coordination with Eliason's formal team of about a dozen Philadelphia staffers. "Those are the real superstars," Westerman stressed.

"The whole Twitter thing for me is really representative of where Comcast is headed with customer service," Westerman said. It's part of a broader effort that includes adding call centers and tens of thousands of customer-service staffers, he emphasized. Yet Twitter is special because it's "a valuable means to grab customer-care data real time and diagnose where outages are...We can very quickly aim our ballistic missiles to the right places."

Westerman recently observed online[22] that "our social-network outreach has generated a wide array of feedback, most of it incredibly useful, some pretty vitriolic. But we need to hear it...For me, it's had the benefit of initiating some great relationships that have been rewarding well beyond the answering of a question or solving a cable problem."

Mike Keliher, the social-media expert at the Provident Partners public-relations and social media consulting firm in St. Paul, Minnesota, said he's "not a big fan of Comcast, and I have had issues with them. But I can't help but love what they're doing with @comcastcares. I have no illusions that this will magically solve all problems and make them the world's most beloved brand. But the fact that Eliason is willing to step into the shitstorm and do the best he can says a lot."

Eliason's effect is magnified by the fact that Twitter users tend to be the Arrington-like "early adopters, thought leaders and online influencers," Keliher told me. "Even though there's a small number of people on Twitter, just geeks playing with their cell phones, this can have a huge snowball effect, a domino effect."

Comcast's efforts "at first glance (consist solely of) putting out online fires," says Dwight Silverman, a tech columnist at the Houston Chronicle. "But it leaves a searchable record. People who were saying, 'Comcast sucks' on websites, blogs and social networks are now saying, 'Hey, this is a pretty cool service.'"

Indeed, online keyword searches for "Comcast," "Eliason" and "comcastcares" now turn up dozens of plaudits from customers, on blogs as well as on Twitter.

---

22 buzzmachine.com/2008/07/28/comments-on-comments-on-comments/#comment-379682

Comcast is even winning over its most prominent critic, Bob Garfield. When I initially interviewed him for this book in early summer, he saw the company's online efforts as a publicity ploy. "They have a dumpster full of grease, and they are out there looking for squeaky wheels," he told me. It's not unlike his own Comcast-service experiences after creating Comcast Must Die, he said. "If I get a little snow on my TV screen now, I have 11 trucks outside my house in an hour."

Garfield's skepticism later eased. He blogged that Comcast had "institutionalized the practice of listening, in live forums around the country but especially on the internet, to resolve individual problems and learn about the (many, gaping) holes in its customer-service operations."[23] This prompted him to declare "victory" on behalf of his Comcast Must Die site and relinquish control of it as it broadened its emphasis beyond Comcast.

As for King, he nearly switched from Comcast to Verizon internet service after lengthy online exchanges with Eliason and much technician tinkering that didn't fix his problem. Something finally took, though, and he stayed with the company. As he put it in a tweet:

ShawnKing: The @comcastcares dude was good. They may have fixed the issue.

But Eliason should not rest easy. King later told me he was "still considering" a move to Verizon because Comcast had only partially fixed his upload issue: "Our upload speeds are acceptable but not nearly as fast as they should be," he observed.

Comcast, meanwhile, has expanded its Twitter presence to include @fancast (associated with a streaming-video site offering movies and TV shows), @comcastdotnet (linked to its consumer website) and @plaxo (associated with Plaxo, the address-book and social-networking service it acquired earlier this year).

---

23 adage.com/garfieldtheblog/post?article_id=130009

The Twitter lesson: Listen to your customers, really listen. Find the conversations that mention you, join them, and turn negatives into positives with zero spin and lots of love.

JetBlue

Jonathan Fields was waiting for a JetBlue flight in New York City when he saw William Shatner saunter up to a nearby gate. The famed "Star Trek" actor "looked exactly like he does on Boston Legal," Fields later told me. As he wrote on his blog: "My first thought is, 'Damn, his piece looks good.'"[24]

Fields, a Twitter user, naturally wanted to tweet about this close encounter with a major celebrity. So he flipped open his Mac laptop, logged on to JetBlue's free Wi-Fi wireless network and wrote:

jonathanfields: JetBlue terminal. William Shatner waiting in pinstripe suit and shades to board flight to Burbank. Why's he flying JetBlue? Free, maybe?

Here's where something unexpected happened, Fields recalled. He checked his email to discover that someone called @jetblue had followed him on Twitter. This alarmed him. His mind raced. Had JetBlue somehow tracked his activity via its registration-required Wi-Fi network? Could they do that? He tweeted:

jonathanfields: Using JetBlue wifi to access twitter, 10 seconds later, I get a follow request from JetBlue on twitter. Half freaked out, half awed.

The explanation, he learned after ditching his flight due to illness and checking his email at home, was not as sinister. This was in his inbox:

---

24 jonathanfields.com/blog/jetblue-twitter-customer-service-or-to-spy

"Hi Jonathan,"

"don't worry—we didn't follow you on Twitter because we saw you on the WiFi (that thought scares even me!)—but because I saw your tweet about William Shatner—my intention was to see if I could DM (direct message) to say something mildly silly about the idea that 'well JetBlue IS on Priceline' or that he could be flying because he likes the Sci Fi Channel."

"Sorry to startle (and Happy Jetting!)"

"Morgan Johnston, Corporate Communications, JetBlue Airways"

Fields had discovered what several thousand others on Twitter already know—JetBlue has been using the microblogging service in a major way.

Johnston, the airline's manager of corporate communications, is a key player in a major customer-service push to revive the once-revered airline after several bad stumbles. The airline is still notorious for mass cancellations and delays in 2007, including one plane stalled at a ramp during a snowstorm for nine hours. Apologetic CEO David Neeleman would later depart in a management purge to remedy continued issues at the 8-year-old carrier. The airline has since redoubled its efforts to make its customers happy, and seems to have found its footing as of this writing.

Johnston boasts that he is a JetBlue "crewmember"—all 100,000 workers, not just traditional flight crews, use that title to emphasize their commitment to their clientele. And unlike traditional communications managers who deal largely with the media, Johnston spends a great deal of his work time interacting directly with customers on the internet.

Twitter happens to be ideal for this—only Johnston didn't realize it at first. "My initial reaction was, 'What's the point of this, exactly?'" he told me. "It's a weird IM service where you don't get IMs." It's only after he began following people with his personal account and engaging in conversations that "it became clear what the point is."

So, earlier this year, "we decided we could be a little more experimental" and set up an official JetBlue identity on Twitter, something that was still unusual for a company to do. "We had a small audience, so if we screwed it up we wouldn't alienate too many people."

JetBlue now uses Twitter to feed its followers travel tips, weather updates and alerts on major flight disruptions and airport closings. In October, it tweeted nonstop about the opening of its shiny new terminal at John F. Kennedy Airport in New York. Johnston's direct interactions with Twitter users tend to have the most impact, though. He has been so eager to mix it up he admits he's overreached on more than one occasion. Some saw him as a bit of a stalker, he said, until realizing he was just trying to be friendly and helpful.

Not all of Johnston's Twitter interactions with his customers have happy endings, he told me, in a show of candor that surprised me. He pointed me to several blog accounts of his Twitter interactions that include one post titled, "JetBlue Delivers a Systematic Customer Service Letdown."[25] That April post (and earlier tweets) detail a traveler's travails with a missing e-ticket, lost baggage, and a baggage handler who brazenly asked for a gratuity.

Johnston said that while he "isn't customer service, I tried to guide (that person) through the process. He was not impressed with the end result, but...we are not always going to win in these situations. It's (still) very important to have the dialogue."

Fields of New York, once reassured that JetBlue wasn't "bugging my backpack," said he was thrilled to learn that "they had someone at JetBlue dedicated to actively engaging on Twitter." As he put it on his blog, "That's pretty damn cool. Cool because they care. And cool because have a clue."

The Twitter lesson: Pay attention to what your customers are saying, and join in when appropriate. They could be startled, but that is a reasonable risk with a potential payoff.

---

25 livingstonbuzz.com/2008/04/28/jetblue-delivers-a-systematic-customer-service-letdown

Zappos

One day, online retailer Zappos gave its San Francisco-area Twitter followers a cryptic command:

zappos: If you r in San Fran area, write "Zappos" on back of left hand w/ marker & twitter @zappos link to picture of it. Why? Details to come

Over the next hours, the company dribbled out more commands: draw a rectangle around the "Zappos"; write your Twitter handle on your right hand; paint your face to look like a zebra (this last one was a joke).

A bit later, the purpose of this exercise was revealed:

zappos: Ok, here's the Zappos twitter experiment! 20 Zappos employees have invaded SF and we want to meet our twitter friends tonight!

zappos: Come to Sky Terrace at Medjool at 2522 Mission 6-9 PM to learn about Zappos culture! Open bar, show "Zappos" on left hand for free drinks.

It was famously outgoing Zappos chief executive Tony Hsieh, a.k.a. @zappos, firing off the tweets from his cell phone, and he wasn't even sure he'd make the gathering. As he toyed with his loyal followers, he was stuck in an airport in another state after being booked on an incorrect flight. It was just like Hsieh to enjoy himself even in moments of high stress.

His company is like that. Staffers are encouraged to act like a fun-loving family. Zappos' 10 ten official "core values" include this item: "create fun and a little weirdness...We don't want to become one of those big companies that feels corporate and boring. We want to be able to laugh out ourselves."

No wonder Zappos—an e-seller of footware, clothes, cookware, electronics, bedding and toys—has embraced the often-zany Twitter in a big way. While its main retail storefront looks much like that of rivals, such as Amazon.com, other parts of the Zappos site show its Twitter-based sense of community.

At twitter.zappos.com, visitors can see a rolling tally of every tweet in the Twitterverse that somehow mentions Zappos. That's where you can see customers gushing about the company's free shipping, free returns, 365-day return policy and superfriendly customer service:

rhjr: Placed 1st Zappos order yesterday, and it arrived today. Have also gotten staff replies through Twitter. I'm officially a big fan.

CasualLavish: My shoes just arrived! I love Zappos.com! Been shopping with them for years. Ordered yesterday they are on my feet today!

The twitter.zappos.com page includes a Twitter guide for those unfamiliar with tweeting.

It also has a listing of every Zappos employee willing to make his or her Twitter account public—454 of them, the last time I checked—as well as rolling tally of Zappos-worker tweets. Those employees are quite active on the service since this is largely how all those fun-loving workers interact.

"We encourage employees to hang out with other employees as much as possible," Hsieh told me. "Twitter is a great way of helping that happen more often," as online exchanges spur offline ones. "The big strength of Twitter is that it encourages people to become more social. Other companies don't value being social."

Hsieh extends this philosophy to his clientele. "Twitter is another way of becoming more human and personal," he said. "It's not a marketing vehicle but a relationship-building vehicle (by) giving our customers a glimpse inside Zappos culture. They feel like they are buying from a friend."

Of course, Zappos might seem a bit too friendly at times. Like Johnston of JetBlue, Hsieh eagerly follows his customers (he tracked more than 18,000 people as of this writing, about as many as were following him). Many of Hsieh's staff have followed suit, adding company customers to those they follow. This triggered a bit of a backlash earlier this year, with tweets like this one:

DougMeacham: When @Zappos CEO started following me it was cool. Now it seems like a new Zappos person follows me every day. Feels forced & kinda creepy!

Hsieh, true to form, asked followers for advice about how to handle this. He got answers like this one:

mediaphyter: @zappos It's a fine line, really. Tell them to engage in conversation first. Otherwise they may get blocked as perceived spambots for Zappos

Meanwhile, Twitter has proven to be "an incredible recruiting tool," said Brian Kalma, a top Hsieh lieutenant who heads up creative services and brand marketing. "I feel since we started using Twitter, we have a much more direct connection to the types of people we want to hire. These are early adopters, innovators."

Zappos Recruiting Manager, Christa Foley, said she has had difficulty finding people with strong marketing and technical backgrounds, for instance, so Twitter has recently been a godsend for her. "Twitter users are marketing people, techie people."

Foley follows "Zappos" mentions on Twitter and tries to identify potential hires. She puts these in a spreadsheet, but doesn't push hard to bring any of them on board. "I don't want to be a headhunter on Twitter, actively spamming people to recruit them," she told me, "I use the soft approach." Only when Twitter users begin following her might she "jokingly mention that we have lots of jobs, and give them my personal email address," she said.

Zappos' Twitter party soured in early November when Hsieh said he was laying off 8 percent of his staff due to "tough economic times." Even in this environment, the Twitterverse united the workers. Their tweets on the Zappos site brimmed with words of comfort and encouragement for each other, a fact Hsieh acknowledged:

Zappos: Sad day, but heartwarming to hear the stories of employees & ex-employees getting together for drinks, true testament to our family culture.

The Twitter lesson: The trend known as social networking can transform your company for the better, externally and internally, if you let it. So embrace it. Savor the adventure!

Whole Foods

Matt Albiniak loves shopping at Whole Foods Market, though this renowned purveyor of natural and organic foods isn't his sole source for groceries. "Their produce really sucks," the St. Paul, Minnesota, man says; he goes to a farmer's market or the competing Kowalski's Market for that. But he'll buy grains and meats at Whole Foods, along with products he and his girlfriend "use on our bodies," because these will have fewer harmful chemicals.

So when Albiniak spotted Whole Foods on Twitter not long ago, he was pretty pumped. He followed @wholefoods right away, and marveled at how the company had managed to engage its customers with seemingly little effort. Whole Foods had drawn more than 2,000 followers after only a few weeks, a remarkable achievement for a corporate user. (A few online plugs from one of Twitter's co-founders, Biz Stone, certainly didn't hurt.) As of October, it had more than 6,000.

It turns out Whole Foods is savvier about Twitter than most. One of its staffers, Slaton Carter, has used it since early 2007. Two others, company blogger Page Brady and website Senior Designer Marla Erwin, are well acquainted with the service and accustomed to laid-back tweeting with their friends in Austin, Texas (where Whole Foods is based). The three have divvied up corporate-tweeting duties on a @wholefoods account, aspiring to the same casual and friendly vibe.

They started with a few rules. They wouldn't use Twitter as an advertising vehicle. The chain doesn't advertise much, in general, preferring to rely on word of mouth among its superloyal clientele, as well as outreach by individual stores that weave themselves into their surrounding neighborhoods.

Another rule: They wouldn't use Twitter to solve customer problems, the way Eliason of Comcast does. The decentralized Whole Foods gives its individual stores wide latitude to deal with such issues, so Carter and his coworkers decided they would refer any client complaints to relevant outlets, or to a customer-care email address.

The three set out to have fun. One ploy: the Favorite Tweet of the Day. They'd scour the Twitterverse for creative or amusing postings that mention Whole Foods, and the authors would score $25 gift cards. (This is a tactic borrowed from Zappos, which is famous for its Twitter-based prize giveaways.)

Albiniak decided to play along. He tweeted the following (in reference to a Whole Foods promotion that gave a local charity a few cents whenever a customer brought in his or her own shopping bags):

malbiniak: @wholefoods i love the bag refund donation to charity. smart on so many levels, but just plain right. great job!

Whole Foods promptly responded:

wholefoods: @malbiniak You earn our second Fav Tweet of the Day, primarily for following us so intently:) DM us with your addy for the $25 card! Thanks

Albiniak later told me he felt delighted in "having the ear of somebody" at such a large company (Whole Foods had about 270 stores across the United States and the United Kingdom as of this writing). "Most companies are so bad in engaging people, in talking with them. Being able to talk to someone at Whole Foods, and have them actually respond in person, as a person, is a little bit impressive."

This encourages him to continue following Whole Foods on Twitter, he said, and to tweet about the company—and not just because he might get a prize. He does admire the firm's environmental principles, and is more than happy to sing their praises in the Twitterverse (even though he doesn't like their produce).

Some customers have complained about the company's gift card ploy, however, calling it crassly commercial, Slaton told me. He noted that the company's approach to Twitter is a work in progress, and will likely morph over a year or so. Individual stores might get their own Twitter accounts, for instance.

What won't change: "We're letting people know there's real people here," he said. When he tweets on the @wholefoods account, for instance, he'll often make it clear that he, not one of his two colleagues, is the one tweeting and will drop in a mention of his personal @tweets identity.

Other companies need to follow suit, said Slaton, who worries they won't. "What I fear is companies getting their public-relations departments involved with Twitter, and diluting its effectiveness," he said. "The reason people are so excited about Twitter is because it is so transparent and open. There's not a lot of pretence."

Whole Foods scored a bit of a publicity coup when it received the following from Kevin Rose, a technology-world celebrity and (as of this writing) one of the Twitter users with the most followers:

kevinrose: @wholefoods I've never talked to a store before, this is odd, hello whole foods

wholefoods: @kevinrose hello:) Think of me as the Hal of natural and organic foods...kidding. Really, live people @twitters @mswinne and @marlaerwin

The Twitter lesson: Enter the Twitterverse on your own terms, and with clear rules, but with customers in mind. Celebrate their creativity, reward it, and they'll love you for it.

Dell

Erin Kotecki Vest needed a new laptop earlier this year, and was leaning towards buying a Macintosh. She said so on Twitter. That's when poor Apple lost her as a customer. The Mac maker doesn't troll Twitter to find and win over potential buyers, but Dell, maker of Windows PCs, often does.

Within minutes of her tweet, Kotecki Vest had heard from several major Twitter users at Dell. One of these, communications officer Richard Binhammer, spent days walking her through her options—almost entirely on Twitter, for all to see.

All the while, she said, Binhammer didn't pressure her. If you want to get a Mac, he told her repeatedly, go for it. She finally placed an order for a hot-pink Dell Inspiron, but the handholding hadn't ended. When the laptop did not arrive at her Los Angeles residence, Dell helped her with shipment tracking. When she had malfunctions with the portable's trackpad, Dell was there to help again.

While her high profile as a family and political blogger may partly account for the royal treatment (she is sometimes offered consumer gear for free, and has been photographed with Barack Obama), she stresses she didn't know Binhammer or anyone else at Dell up to that point.

Binhammer, who is perhaps the company's most prominent Twitter user, said he did not "act as a salesperson but more as a guide" in his interactions with Kotecki Vest. "I didn't get on Twitter to sell computers."

But that's precisely what Binhammer has done, again and again as @RichardatDELL, in Twitter-based conversations with friends, business acquaintances and complete strangers.

This is one indication of how Twitter and other social-media services are changing how Dell does business. While a sprinkling of Twitter-related sales may seem miniscule when compared to the tens of millions of dollars Dell generates in sales every year, it is proof of how this famous computer maker is connecting with its customers in creative ways.

It wasn't always so. The company became associated with the buzz-phrase "Dell Hell" in 2005 after prominent blogger Jeff Jarvis wrote in excruciating detail about his problems with defective Dell hardware and his horrendous difficulty in dealing with the company about this.[26] (He ended up switching to Apple gear.) Dell later acknowledged it did not pay much attention to blog chatter and other online buzz about its products and services.

By 2006, though, the company was paying attention. It initially reached out to those with technical issues, and later began keeping track of all online chatter about the company. It now monitors social networks, and actively engages those who are talking about its gear.

"As a Fortune 500 company, we're getting our heads around the fact that the world won't come to you," Bob Pearson, Vice President of Communities and Conversations, told me in a phone interview. "You have to be relevant in consumer conversations wherever those happen—Facebook, Orkut, Bebo, Twitter, Pownce, MySpace. We are on a lot of these."

Dell's site links prominently to its various online outposts. These include a growing network of blogs, which were the firm's first prominent foray into social media, as well as the Second Life virtual-reality realm, Dell's own user forums, and its Ideastorm site that takes user ideas. The company offers a web-based "conversations" hub for customers who want to "discuss, review, suggest, compliment, complain or comment" using Twitter or any of the other services.[27]

The company even sanctioned employee use of Facebook early on, and in July broadened this policy to include other services, like the Flickr photo-sharing site and the YouTube video-sharing site along with Twitter and other microblogging services. By then, some 40 staffers were using Twitter in an official capacity[28]—including about 20 in Japan and other offshore locations.

---

26 buzzmachine.com/archives/cat_dell.html
27 dell.com/conversations
28 direct2dell.com/one2one/archive/2008/07/10/Dell-Opens-Up-Social-Me
dia-Sites-to-All-Employees.aspx

Binhammer told me, though, that he "went on Twitter, to be perfectly truthful, with a lot of skepticism. What was I going to say on it in 140 characters?"

Turns out, quite a lot. Like other successful corporate Twitter denizens, Binhammer has cracked the 1,000-follower threshold while also following plenty of people so that two-way conversations can easily take place.

That's important, Pearson told me. "One of the indicators of intensity on Twitter is if you look at followers and the followed, and see that the ratio is one-to-one. Some people have lots of followers but don't follow anyone. That is a form of digital narcissism. It's a sign you aren't connecting with others."

Dell also has begun using Twitter to sell its stuff. In early 2008 it created @DellOutlet as an offshoot of the Dell Outlet site that sells refurbished computers and electronics. Using a Twitter account to hawk merchandise instead of engage in conversations was a cautious experiment, Pearson now acknowledges.

"It was a perfect example of an experiment that doesn't cost anything, but it was totally, 100-percent up to the community to decide if it's relevant," he said. "If they say no, we don't do it. They vote by their participation, and it became pretty clear that they want it."

With solid sales at @DellOutlet, the company followed up with @DellHomeOffers and, a bit later, @DellSmBizOffers. Earlier this year, this Twitter activity accounted for more than $500,000 in revenue—not bad for a bunch of tweets.[29]

Dell uses Twitter to communicate with the media, too. In early August, it took questions from reporters and customers about its latest mobile products, and tweeted the replies via its @Digital_Nomads account. This was part of a joint press event in San Francisco, New Delhi and London.[30]

---

29 direct2dell.com/one2one/archive/2008/06/21/dell-and-twitter.aspx
30 dell.com/content/topics/global.aspx/corp/pressoffice
/en/2008/2008_08_11_rr_000?c=us&l=en&s=corp

Dell's presence on Twitter goes well beyond what I've outlined here, and even what Dell lists on its own site.[31] A directory of Dell-related Twitter accounts (with information that Binhammer provided) can be found on the Fluent Simplicity site.[32]

Meanwhile, @RichardatDELL and Kotecki Vest (who tweets as @QueenofSpain) remain friends in the Twitterverse. Here's one recent exchange:

RichardatDELL: @queenofspain most subdued pic I have seen you use yet :-)

QueenofSpain: @RichardatDELL lol. there is one of me with my pink dell somewhere....

RichardatDELL: @QueenofSpain with your pink dell and obama? let me see

QueenofSpain: @RichardatDELL lol. sorry to disappoint just ME and the pink dell. Speaking of dells...My parents need one....talk to me

The Twitter lesson: The Twitterverse is a wondrously versatile realm, so use it in lots of ways. Burnish your brand, make a few bucks, help customers, and make friends. Have fun!

---

31 dell.com/content/topics/global.aspx/community/dell_on_twitter
32 blog.fluentsimplicity.com/twitter-brand-index/dell

3 More Companies on Twitter

When researching this book, I was struck by the sheer variety of companies migrating to Twitter, and the wide range of uses they found for it. This is partly a testament to those companies' ingenuity, and partly a result of Twitter's simplicity—this makes it deliciously malleable in the business sense.

This chapter is something of a grab bag, as a result. Some companies use Twitter for a two-way conversation with clients, while others use it only for one-way broadcasting. Some project businesslike personas while others strive to be human, often with humor. Companies of all sizes, ranging from corporate titans to small family-run concerns, are profiled here. Some are members of the journalism industry, which is dear to my heart.

If you're figuring out how to use Twitter at your firm, this chapter will teach you a lot.

The Internet-Video Provider

No company is more preoccupied with Twitter-verse mentions of its name than Blip.tv.

The New York City-based video firm, known mainly for TV-style programs distributed over the internet, scours Twitter continually. "Every single day and throughout the day, our content team monitors every single mention of Blip.tv on Twitter," said Dina Kaplan, a company co-founder and its Chief Operating Officer.

At 11 a.m., summaries of such Twitter mentions, good and bad, are distributed all over the small office (the company has about 20 people in the city's SoHo district). This is largely how the firm can see how it's doing, and what problems need to be addressed.

"Twitter has enabled us to be closer to our audience than any other tool I can imagine," Kaplan told me. "It is an unbelievably valuable tool for business for learning what we do right and what we should do better. In some respects, it helps guide the development of the entire company. I could not even put a price tag on how valuable Twitter has been to us as we grow as a business."

Last spring, for instance, Twitter users complained about uploaded videos taking too long to "transcode" from the QuickTime format to the Flash format used on Blip.tv. "Because we're monitoring Twitter, we noticed this immediately," Kaplan said. "We doubled the number of transcoders, which we ordered that day, and within a week they were all in place. We turned around what could have been a big problem into something positive."

"People are stunned when you do this," she said. "They say, 'Wow, someone is listening to me. A company is actually listening to me.'"

In another case, Blip.tv users on the West Coast were having trouble playing videos due to slow internet performance, Kaplan said. "We were able to catch that probably within the hour because of Twitter. It might otherwise take months to catch on. You might be in a bar five months later, and a content creator might tell you he had been having an issue." But by then, it's much too late, she said.

Twitter is invaluable for alerting users about technical problems or updates, too:

bliptv: at 10:30 am this morning, we experienced network connectivity issues at our primary NYC datacenter.

bliptv: we pushed out significant updates to our flash/h.264 transcode tool this week, including real-time conversion monitoring!

Twitter also is handy for promoting Blip.tv-based content:

Bliptv: Dina Prioste explains how your two nostrils are tied to the two sides of your brain, demonstrates breathing hack http://is.gd/nCx

Bliptv: this howto/lifehack video is kinda creepy and kinda awesome: "how to grow grass in someone's keyboard" http://Blip.tv/file/939841

The company finds Twitter so effective because "it caters to the early-adopter audience that is inclined to use Blip.tv," Kaplan explained. "Those are the people who give friends recommendations on which services to use. Those are the folks we need to keep happy."

The Twitter lesson: Obsessing about what your customers are saying about you in the Twitterverse could be one of the keys to a thriving business. Wake up and pay attention!

The Tax-Advice Company

Most who see the H&R Block name will associate it with the company's physical chain of tax-help help outlets in strip malls. That's a problem, says Amy Worley, the company's Director of Digital Marketing, because H&R Block is lately a lot more than that.

Worley has been on a crusade to publicize the company's digital offerings, including its TaxCut options for doing taxes online or using the company's TaxCut desktop software. These comprised a full 40 percent of H&R Block's business as of last summer, but most don't understand this, she said. "We're out to change those perceptions," she said.

Twitter has figured prominently in this effort. Worley is a veteran as corporate tweeters go, having used the service since June 2007, so she grasped that it could be a vital forum for educating its customers. The company does this partly by pumping out its tax tips:

HRBlock: Moved because of your job? You may be able to deduct some of the moving costs.

HRBlock: Did you get a smaller refund than expected? You can give your W-4 a checkup now to help avoid surprises in April.

Beyond just broadcasting information, the company has been eager to answer customers' questions. Twitter works best with two-way interactions, and Worley clearly understands this. The company talks with its Twitter fans nonstop:

HRBlock: We've had amazing interactions w/ customers on Twitter. We've provided customer support, eased stress, found jobs & made friends.

H&R Block also has set up digital outposts on Facebook, MySpace, YouTube and other such places, "but Twitter has provided the richest level of engagement," Worley said. "It provides interaction with customers that is unmatched." And simply by being present on Twitter, H&R Block makes folks understand that it isn't solely a brick-and-mortar entity, she said.

Twitter now serves many roles for the company, she added: "It's a customer-support tool, a public-relations tool, and a product-development tool with feedback from customers on what they like and don't like" about the company's online services and desktop software.

H&R Block scored its biggest PR coup earlier this year when Robert Scoble, the famous technology evangelist and hugely prolific blogger and Twitterer, happened to be visiting an H&R Block retail store in late March. He tweeted this fact and H&R Block promptly responded. Here's the exchange:

Scobleizer: doing taxes at H&R Block. I am braced for bad news.

HRBlock: @Scobleizer Sending happy tax prep vibes your way. Make sure you tweet back and let us know how everything went

Scobleizer: @HRBlock is on Twitter and is fast. There is your Twitter business model.

A couple of days later, Scoble tweeted again:

Scobleizer: @antioniocapo HRBlock twittered WHILE I was in their office getting taxes done. That was amazing.

Though the number of Twitter users remains relatively small by internet standards, she said, people like Scoble have "the influence to evangelize" a brand. That's just what he later did. Here is an exchange with Houston Chronicle tech writer Dwight Silverman:

dsilverman: besides @jetblue, @comcastcares & @lionelatdell, any other companies doing customer service on twitter?

Scobleizer: @dsilverman @hrblock is a company on Twitter.

"The value of every interaction we have on Twitter is the opportunity to demonstrate that H&R Block is an advocate for the taxpayer," Worley later told me. "We're here to be a partner—a coach—to help our customers achieve their tax goals. We didn't seek out the encounter with Scoble; we just saw him mention our brand and we responded. But that interaction was especially valuable simply because of his following. The interaction took place in front of a large audience, so the brand impact was greater."

The Twitter lesson: Looking to remake your business for a digital age? The Twitterverse could be one of the crucial ingredients, so embrace this realm and all its influential folks.

The Public-Radio Reporter

Public-radio reporter Jon Gordon works in his Alameda, California, single-car garage, which has a concrete floor and a washer and dryer that churn nearby. For a journalist needing to be connecting with humanity, this arrangement has been isolating over the years, he said.

Twitter has lately been an antidote, rescuing him from his journalistic exile and putting him in the midst of a virtual throng. Like a growing number of other journalists, Gordon has seized on Twitter as a new and effective way to develop sources, solicit story ideas, make friends and partake in conversations that have helped make him a better reporter.

Gordon, who produces a brief, daily "Future Tense" technology show for St. Paul, Minnesota-based Minnesota Public Radio (MPR) and the American Public Media radio network, was frantic for a segment subject earlier this year, so he asked his hundreds of Twitter followers for ideas. One follower suggested:

red_beecher: @jongordon: Interview with the voice behind Phoenix? (Whoever it is that does the probe's twittering, I mean)

This turned out to be a great idea because @MarsPhoenix, the Twitter identity associated with NASA's Mars Phoenix lander, had become one of the most popular with more than 36,000 followers at press time. Gordon's interview with Veronica McGregor,[33] a NASA staffer responsible for the tweeting, also proved popular.[34]

Gordon said his Twitter followers have become a "sounding board, an informal editorial board." Yet he's wary about "ascribing too much importance to this one group of people. They are a really important and interesting resource, but it's just a few hundred people. You don't want to give this one group of people too much influence over what you do."

Gordon (@jongordon) is part of a Twitter surge at MPR, in a pattern being seen at print publications and broadcast outlets across the country as the mainstream-media business increasingly grasps the service's value. More than a dozen reporters, editors, producers and technical staffers at MPR had Twitter accounts as of this writing, making it perhaps the most Twitter-hip media outlet in the Twin Cities.

MPR showed signs of struggling with this nascent medium, though. Senior blogger Bob Collins, in particular, displayed a love-hate relationship with Twitter. Early in the year, he scornfully called tweets "digital

---

33 twitter.com/VeronicaMcG
34 publicradio.org/columns/futuretense/2008/06/25.shtml

spitballs." Later, he tried embracing the service and, for a time, became a prolific tweeter (loosely associated with his employer) with snarky tweets like this one:

bcollinsmn: Who do I need to talk to in order to get a fatwah on Barbara Walters? It's like listening to your parents discuss their sex lives.

He soon became disenchanted, however:

bcollinsmn: Resolution: No more Twitter during working hours. Problem: There are no non-working hours.

At one point Collins let his MPR-related Twitter account languish while switching to a personal account stripped of any MPR mention or connection, effectively muzzling himself as an MPR advocate. "I have no interest in being MPR Twitter," he wrote at one point.

Collins later resumed MPR tweeting but maintained a strict demarcation between his work and home accounts—something of an anomaly in a Twitterverse where the personal and professional tend to blend.

MPR, meanwhile, had to wrest an @MPRmn account from an outsider who had created an unofficial MPR-headline service.[35] This rogue MPR account had not impressed MPR fans like Erica Mauter of Minneapolis Metblogs:

swirlspice: I don't know who @MPRmnfan is, but thinking you're doing the public a service by dumping MPR's (news headlines) into Twitter is laughable.

But what MPR did with the account once taking control of it in August did not impress Mauter, either. That's right: it turned the account into a headline service (and one that languished as of early October after attracting little interest). MPR took a similarly unimaginative approach with a Twitter account associated with its popular-music station The Current, Mauter observed.[36]

---

35 minneapolis.metblogs.com/2008/08/25
/minnesota-public-radio-vs-twitter-account-squatter
36 minneapolis.metblogs.com/2008/02/11/the-current-on-twitter

"I'm not a fan of (headline) dumping, by anyone," Mauter told me. "If you're going to tweet other stuff in addition to that, that's one thing, but if that's all you're going to do, BOO."

The Twitter lesson: Twitter can have a transformative effect at news organizations that embrace its two-way nature and learn how to connect with those who use their content.

The Television Reporter

Nearby CBS affiliate WCCO-TV also has embraced Twitter. Like numerous other news organizations, the Minneapolis-based TV station has a Twitter feed to push out breaking-news bulletins and updates. Unlike most such feeds, which spew material automatically, @WCCO-breaking is run by actual humans and has a personality, something that Twitter users appreciate.

WCCOBreaking: Hikers missing then found in Alaskan wilderness... now missing again?! We're not making this up!! More details shortly at www.wcco.com

WCCOBreaking: Forgive my indulgence. But I'm very sorry to share that WCCO's Bob Rainey died this morning of cancer. He was a dear friend & fine co-worker

WCCO reporter Jason DeRusha, meanwhile, has flourished as a Twitter-using journalist, which comes naturally for him since he has been an internet geek all his adult life and has relished services like MySpace, Facebook and LinkedIn. "I started using Twitter socially with friends," he told me. "It was not as a way to push my message or my work. But when I got a good chunk of people following me, I could throw out questions about stories."

Initially working as a night reporter at WCCO, DeRusha found Twitter invaluable for getting story material on his ever-tight deadlines. For a story about allergies caused by mold on Christmas trees, for instance, he put out a query to his then-80 followers:

DeRushaJ: Anyone have an allergy that makes you go nuts because of a live Christmas tree? Email me...

Minutes later, he received a reply from a woman who had to wear gloves when touching her Christmas tree. This made DeRusha's story, which up to that point only had tiresome elements such as an interview with a health expert and footage from a Christmas-tree lot.

DeRushaJ would eventually take charge of WCCO's "Good Question" segment, which takes a daily stab at questions that are uppermost on viewers' minds or, at least, get the watchers thinking. Twitter is a good tool for this, he said, because it imposes focus and discipline by forcing him to formulate the question of the day in 140 characters or less. He can then blast it out to his Twitter followers for their input:

DeRushaJ: Help me with tonight's Good Question: Economy's a bust; box offices are booming. Why? Are you spending on movies?

DeRushaJ: Tonight's Good Question: When you lose weight, where does it go? Pee it out? Poop? Sweat?

"Their online feedback helps shape the way I put together my stories," DeRusha said.

The Twitter lesson: In the Twitterverse, the old broadcast-only media model is old hat. Open-minded journalists are learning to embrace and exploit a two-way online realm.

The Theme and Water Park

Holiday World and Splashin' Safari claims it was the first theme park to blog (it started doing that three years ago). Now it says it's the first such family complex to microblog via Twitter.

The Santa Claus, Indiana-based facility is always a bit ahead of the social-media curve, as such facilities go, courtesy of its web-savvy Director of Public Relations, Paula Werne.

Back in 2006, she was looking to build buzz for a big new rollercoaster, the Voyage, that would debut that Thanksgiving. Her "Holiblog" proved perfect for providing construction updates and telling all the fun little tales that newspaper reporters and travel writers never seemed to put in their articles.

The Holiblog got lots of attention around the world because roller-coaster diehards were closely following news about the Voyage, which is still widely regarded as one of the top wooden roller coasters in the world. (Werne recalls that web traffic during the Voyage's debut crashed a local TV station's site as it tried to provide streaming-video coverage.)

So when Werne heard about Twitter earlier this year, she thought it would be the "perfect companion piece for the blog." She saw it as an effective way "to communicate with the guests in the park, and to tell little stories. I could write about something a kid said that was funny, talk about the weather, or let people know that a certain ride would be late."

HolidayWorld: Fox 7 was just here to do a story about the hot day and what folks do to cool off. The reporter didn't sweat a drop. Amazing.

HolidayWorld: Spent the pm with two great guys from the Chicago Tribune. Got them on The Voyage. Mike said, "I left my dignity out there in the woods."

HolidayWorld: I just got an email from someone whose cousin told her The Voyage goes 150 miles per hour. She was fact checking. Smart girl.

Twitter has proven convenient, Werne said, because "it's so easy to send a message from my phone, and I enjoy it tremendously."

She adds that her Twitter identity has attracted more publicity for the park because tweets about upcoming attractions are being reprinted on rollercoaster-enthusiast websites such as CoasterBuzz, which seized on the following:

HolidayWorld: We had a meeting to discuss naming ideas for one of our 2009 projects. We always call the meeting the "Name Game." Ugh. It's so not a game!

The Twitter lesson: If you're in a fun-loving line of work, the Twitter-verse could be the perfect complement! Consider it an online extension of what you've been doing already.

The Electronic-Book Publisher

Adam Engst tweets as @adamengst. He also tweets as @TidBITS and @TakeControl, the names of a technology-themed online newsletter and e-book publishing house he runs with his wife, Tonya.

It's a crucial distinction, Engst said, because his personal Twitter account gets the most traffic by far. As of fall, Adam had more than 1,400 followers on his personal account, but fewer than 80 on the Take Control account and fewer than 500 on the TidBITS account. (Tonya just over 300 at @tonyaengst, but she maintains a lower profile than her husband.)

The lesson here: "Companies need to have human faces," Engst said. "I've been saying this since the beginning of the internet. A company that isn't comfortable with a human face shouldn't bother" (using services like Twitter). "Businesses have no excuse not using Twitter, it's so simple. But do it with a human face."

Apple is a case in point, said Engst, whose longtime TidBITS online newsletter and Take Control e-books focus on Macintosh computers and other Apple technologies. Apple has not embraced Twitter but could be doing so effectively, Engst believes.

"If Steve Jobs actually used Twitter, he'd have seventeen zillion follow-ers," said Engst, referring to Apple's famously secretive and enigmatic Chief Executive.

The Engsts blend business and the personal in their tweeting, which comes naturally for them since they run their relatively small publishing concern out of their Ithaca, New York, home while juggling cooking and child duties along with biking and running. Adam is well known among his Twitter followers for posting the particulars of his athletic and cooking exploits. He's famously systematic:

adamengst: The trick with cooking good food for dinner is making a menu and shopping on the weekend. End-of-day is tough for thinking of what to make.

adamengst: Our secret shortcut: We make menus/shopping lists and keep them each week. We can now go back 18 years for ideas of what to make in season.

He's come in for a bit of ribbing for this, from me and others:

jojeda: @bynkii @shawnking He cooks. He runs. He superorganizes projects. He moonlights as a cowled crimefighter. @adamengst makes us all look bad:/

ShawnKing: @jojeda @bynkii I know! Which is why, secretly and in our heart of hearts, we all *loathe* @adamengst...

All kidding aside, @adamengst is a must-follow for Mac-loving Twitter users since it's a window into one of the best Mac minds. Twitter has become valuable to the Engsts (and especially to Adam) in their work, too. As he writes in his TidBITS article "Confessions of a Twitter convert":[37]

"I'm eating a hearty meal of crow (roasted, with garlic and rosemary) today, since I'm here to tell you how interesting and downright useful I've found Twitter to be since being turned onto it properly..."

"My initial reaction to Twitter was that it was utterly inane. Frankly, I put much of the blame on Twitter itself, asking as it does, 'What are you doing?' as a way of prompting people to post 140-character messages. For the most part, as I acerbically noted before, no one cares what you're doing. However, that's not entirely true, and what I missed in my quick and disdainful overview is that a certain number of people do

---

37 db.tidbits.com/article/9228

care what you're doing, as long as it's interesting, funny, or relevant in some other way. And here's the other thing—they, not you, get to decide if you're interesting, funny, or relevant."

The Twitter lesson: Never forget your company is made up of humans, and project that humanity into the Twitterverse. If you do this well, others will respond and embrace you.

The Comic-Panel Artists

Liza Schmalcel and Bruce Evans, known as "Nitrozac" and "Snaggy," have lampooned the tech world in their Joy of Tech[38] comic strip for going on a decade (while catering in other geeky products, like propeller beanies and customized cartoon portraits rendered digitally and physically). So when Twitter arrived, they embraced it and had fun with it.

One Joy of Tech strip has tips of what not to tweet. Examples: "cheating on girlfriend at the Motel 6" and "putting a bit of poison in husband's soup."[39] Another panel teases tech journalist and Twitter superuser Robert Scoble, who is being saved from alien abductors by Arnold the Terminator. "Just a sec!" the Scobleizer tells Ah-nuld. "I've got to Twitter this!"[40]

The Vancouver Island, British Columbia, residents love to use Twitter (as @nitrozac and @snaggy). When I asked them to tell me what effect the service has had on their thriving company, dubbed Geek Culture, they responded with a blend of humor and seriousness:

- Flushed all productivity down the toilet ;-)

- The viral spread of links to our comics has been great.

- People using Nitrozac-drawn avatars has led to more business for her portraits.

---

38 joyoftech.com
39 geekculture.com/joyoftech/joyarchives/939.html
40 geekculture.com/joyoftech/joyarchives/1077.html

- Encouraged people to order propeller beanies, as well as facilitated some customer comments/service.

- Encouraged contacts with other professionals and peers. We arranged to have a comic in Macworld magazine via twittering with editor Jason Snell.

- The occasional comic idea will result from a tweet or Twitter in general.

- It's a way to interact with fans on a more personal level.

- Use of Twitter gets us into books about the use of Twitter :P

The Twitter lesson: The Twitterverse is a good place to energize an already-loyal fan base, drum up new business, get ideas for fresh projects, and not take life too seriously.

The Candy Purveyor

Green M&Ms have long been reputed to have sex-enhancing qualities.[41] Earlier this year, M&M maker Mars Snacks opted to embrace and not ignore this juicy rumor, building a publicity campaign around the character of "Ms. Green."[42]

It declared: "What is it about The Green Ones®? Legend has it The Green Ones® are an aphrodisiac; rumors of their special powers have been circulating since the '70s."

Twitter figured prominently into this campaign—alongside a limited-edition release of green candies that were promoted heavily in TV commercials and on a special website. The idea was to create "a whole green community (where visitors could) learn about the urban myth," said Ryan Bowling, a Mars public-relations manager for its snack brands.

---

41 snopes.com/risque/aphrodisiacs/mandms.asp
42 prnewswire.com/mnr/mars/31278

The female candy character threw out tweets like these:

msgreen: Things are really heating up this V-Day season! Details about my upcoming personal appearances are on their way. Stay tuned.

msgreen: Hey. Can you guess who my favorite all-time football player is? If you said Mean Joe Greene, give yourself a great big kiss!

Ms. Green tweeted from January through March "in a quirky, sassy way," Bowling said. "It's a unique way to raise the profile of Ms. Green."

This is the sort of Twitter use that makes some veteran users' eyes roll. For Twitter purists, the service is all about genuine interactions between real people, and not fabrications foisted on the Twitterverse by corporate America and its Madison Avenue associates. But many more such publicity campaigns are likely to come.

In fact, Mars Candy has created a separate @mmsracing identity focused on the "Red" M&M character and the snack company's affiliation with NASCAR racer Kyle Busch.

mmsracing: Hi, this is Red: M&M'S® Racing's #1 Fan! I'll be here twittering about racing, Kyle Busch & the colorful #18 car for all of racing season

mmsracing: Did you see the way Kyle handled his car in Daytona? Wow...such skill. Such finesse! Such talent! I'm still in awe. Kyle #1!!!

"All marketers are looking at social media, and wanting to try out new things," Bowling said. "Twittering about M&Ms is a way to do that."

The Twitter lesson: Whether a cartoon frontman or frontwoman for a candy product can make it in the keep-it-real Twitterverse remains to be seen, but there's no harm in trying!

The Business-Services Provider

San Francisco-based Salesforce (like Blip.tv and others) is obsessed with tracking what its customers are saying on Twitter. Staffer Joseph Kingsley has elevated this almost to an art.

Kingsley is an internet "community manager" for Successforce.com, an online gathering place for Salesforce clientele. These are typically large companies that use the Salesforce suite of CRM (short for "customer relationship management") online services to manage complex commercial operations.

This isn't sexy, like other topics discussed on Twitter, but the Twitter-verse is replete with Salesforce and Successforce mentions—and you can bet Kingsley catches all of them. He has a system.

He uses Yahoo Pipes.[43] This is a handy Yahoo service for scouring all corners of the web via a series of automated "feeds," and then pulling the information into a centralized spot for sorting, filtering and organizing. Via Yahoo Pipes, Kingsley keeps track of Saleforce-related chatter on Twitter and other tech-buzz-filled sites, such as Flickr, YouTube, Digg, Techmeme and FriendFeed (he's adding new ones all the time).

In this way, "I plug myself into a live stream of updates" from all over the Twitterverse and the rest of cyberspace, Kingsley told me. This lets him respond to Salesforce clients with lightning speed. That surprises them because they don't expect a business-services company "to be talking with them on Twitter...and by reacting to those conversations in real time, I have a huge role in shaping where those conversations go."

Kingsley (who tweets as @successforce and @kingsley2) says his Pipes experiment has opened his eyes. "I had no idea so many people were talking about our brand in so many different places. It is a huge revelation."

His work has also made him a bit of a social-media star with prominent blog mentions.[44]

---

43 pipes.yahoo.com/pipes
44 churchofthecustomer.com/blog/2008/04/keeping-up-with.html

The Las Vegas Casino

Visiting Vegas? Wondering what to do with your time? The @Vegas-Concierge wants to help. It's a service of MGM MIRAGE, the company known for its MGM Grand Las Vegas hotel and more than a dozen other swanky facilities around the country.

Meant for Twitter users on holiday in Las Vegas while tracking their tweets on their cell phones, @VegasConcierge spits out a steady stream of suggestions:

VegasConcierge: Excalibur is offering free Blackjack lessons today starting at 11:30a.m. and free Craps lessons starting at noon.

VegasConcierge: If you're up late this morning, a pretty unique spot to go for food and entertainment is the House of Blues for their Gospel Brunch

VegasConcierge: Wedding Crashers movie playing on the beach at Mandalay Bay Friday. FREE Admission

MGM Mirage hatched the idea in a partnership with Edelman, its social-media advisor, and decided from the start not to focus its tweeting only on its Las Vegas properties, said Lou Ragg, MGM MIRAGE executive director of internet marketing. He sees the Twittering as one way to "really get us more involved in social media."

The Twitter lesson: The Twitterverse needs to be useful, and you can help. Give others information that can help them enjoy themselves and make better consumer decisions.

The Music-Hardware Maker

Consumers with electronics problems are sick and tired of waiting on hold for help, and they find online user forums confusing and intimidating, Thomas Meyer believes. He is the public-relations manager for Sonos, a maker of high-end audio gear that is billed as supersimple to use. Meyer wants Sonos customer service to be painless, too.

So he and his colleagues recently began using Twitter to zero in on customer complaints and try resolving them. The Sonos staffers are following internet-hip consumers who are getting in the habit of venting on Twitter, Facebook and other social-networking portals, Meyer said. They find this "quick, painless and definitely better than waiting on hold for someone to pick up a phone."

For this reason, Meyer said, "We need to open up as many paths of communication as possible to ensure that the consumer feels like they can get the support they need, that they can get their question answered."

Twitter interventions can be quite effective, even when they do not unfold flawlessly, he said, recalling one unhappy-customer tweet earlier this year:

fxshaw: Very unhappy that rhapsody on sonos is not working...having music meltdown...

This was a reference to a Rhapsody online-streaming music service, which runs on Sonos hardware.

"Unfortunately, (the customer) had this experience very late last night and posted about it after midnight," Meyer recalled. "But, in the morning, one of our consumer-support guys saw it and immediately replied to his tweet and encouraged him to call us. We got to him seven hours or so later—because we don't have 24/7 support—which stinks, but we are attempting whenever feasible to go the extra mile to reach out to our customers to better their experience."

Turns out that customer is a pretty high-profile person: He is Frank Shaw, a partner at Waggener Edstrom Worldwide, the global public-relations agency and head of the firm's Microsoft-related P.R. efforts.

When I recently asked Shaw about that Twitter exchange (which was the second time Sonos had reached out to him in response to one of his tweets) he said he was impressed and "pleasantly surprised" by the firm's Twitter-centric outreach efforts.

"Sonos understands its customer base really well," Shaw told me. "The people who tend to buy a Sonos system are relatively technically literate. Those are the same people who are most active in social media. Twitter is close to a direct fit for Sonos, so responding to their customers via that specific channel is smart."

Oddly, Sonos didn't have an official Twitter identity as of this writing. But a tech-support staffer did tweet publicly as @davethemusicguy. Sonos was mulling whether to deploy a @Sonos account as of this writing.

The Twitter lesson: The Twitterverse can be a fine way to tap into your customer base and render assistance if needed. Some customers might be big shots, so pay attention!

The iPhone-Software Publisher

Graeme Thickins walked a fine line when he fashioned a Twitter identity for DoApp, a Minnesota-based publisher of software for Apple's iPhone. He had to pump the firm's applications, including a myTo-Dos program for keeping task lists, and a playful Magic-8-Ball-like myAnswers application. At the same time, the marketing manager wanted to avoid irking web-hip Twitter users, who sometimes balk at anything cravenly commercial.

So, between plugs for DoApp's wares, he used his @DoApp identity as a sort of news feed to keep followers apprised of developments in iPhone application development—which, as of last summer, was a superhot subject in the consumer-technology universe.

In an effort to engage his customers, Thickins also scoured the Twitterverse for mentions of DoApp and got permission to post some of the more interesting tweets. DoApp clients were finding all kinds of interesting uses for the myLite program, which is a combination flashlight, strobe, party light, emergency flasher and rock-concert lighter (it has a virtual facsimile of a cigarette lighter, flickering flame and all). Thickins documented nearly two dozen such uses for the hugely popular app:

DoApp: #6 consumer use of our myLite app—well, actually, a *professional* use ! ... radiologist setting it to red for use in the x-ray room :-)

DoApp: myLite use #12: WVA medic used emerg flasher at festival at night "so other members of rescue and fire could find me in dark sea of people"

Twitter also proved priceless for communication with the media, Thickins said. When a Rochester, Minnesota, newspaper wanted to write about DoApp, the reporter contacted him via Twitter, and not via email or the phone. With more and more tech journalists getting on Twitter, he said, tech companies have to be using the service. Though DoApp has a presence on Facebook, Twitter has far surpassed it in importance.

"It's a mandatory tool for any internet company today—and certainly for anyone like us involved in a rapidly moving market like iPhone apps," said Thickins, who left DoApp in a full-time capacity late this year, but still consults for the firm. "It's something we just can't not do."

The Twitter lesson: If you're an up-and-coming business, the Twitter-verse can be the place to promo your products and cultivate a following. Just don't be too commercial.

The Internet-Software Publisher

When Andrew Sinkov suggested creating a Twitter identity for Evernote, the internet-software company where he works as Marketing Director, he ran into initial resistance.

At the time, the Silicon Valley company was undergoing a radical transformation. Its PC-only note-making software was being supplanted by versions for Macs along with PCs, as well as a web-based Evernote incarnation and options for using mobile devices. Amid all of this activity at a firm filled with hard-nosed engineers, something seemingly trivial like Twitter was not seen as a big priority.

The reaction was, "OK, this is kind of a waste of time," Sinkov said. "But I felt this was exactly what a company in the Web 2.0 space should be doing."

Evernote eventually became one of the more successful instances of a company adopting a Twitter identity. It boasted about 6,000 Twitter followers as of this writing, which is very, very good for a corporate account. This is partly because Evernote's software is a darling of the web-tech set, the very power users who flock to Twitter in the first place.

For this reason, Twitter has proven invaluable for identifying problems with its software (which is continually undergoing changes). If a bug crops up, Sinkov said, Evernote will hear about it, almost instantly. "I can take bug reports to our engineers, and in a number of cases they are able to resolve them within basically hours. This means I am getting at problems before the general population has a sense of them."

evernote: We think we've fixed the disappearing menubar clipper icon in Evernote for Mac with this latest update. Fingers crossed.

evernote: Evernote for Windows users, make sure to update. We released a new version last night with some bug fixes.

Sinkov also conducts little user polls on Twitter. Once he asked Evernote's followers how they use the software and received more than 80 responses. Unlike other companies like Comcast, however, Evernote does not respond directly to Twitter users. "I ask other folks to do this," Sinkov said, while the Twitter account serves as "the voice of Evernote."

evernote: Hey Evernote for iPhone users. Do you have any cool tips, tricks, or use cases? Reply @evernote and we'll put them on our blog. Thanks!

The Twitter lesson: A popular product will help you build a Twitter-verse following, but you have to nurture it. Keep users informed, and get them involved. They will respond.

4 Twitter and Public Relations

Public-relations agencies fill a vital role in business by telling companies how to behave in public—online as well as off. And because P.R. agencies tend to be internet fanatics, many have embraced Twitter and encouraged their business-world clients to do likewise.

In fact, agencies that don't use Twitter are increasingly seen as oddities. Todd Defren, a P.R. star at the bicoastal SHIFT Communications agency, puts it this way in a blog post: "Get into Twitter or Get Outta Public Relations?"[45] David Alston of online-tracking firm Radian6 (see Chapter Six) writes on his TweetPR blog, "Digital PR? No Twitter account is like no fax number in the 80's."[46]

No wonder I have devoted a full chapter to P.R. agencies and their Twitter-related work.

---

45 pr-squared.com/2008/04
/get_into_twitter_or_get_outta.html
46 tweetpr.com/?p=16

Tweeting to Mommies

Paull Young is a Twitter veteran, partly out of necessity. When the Australian moved to New York City for a public-relations job in 2007, his tweets were one of the main ways his family back home kept up on his Big American Adventure.

His agency, Converseon, focuses on social media (including blogs and social-networking services like Twitter), so everyone in the office uses Twitter to some extent, Young said. Last Christmas, the firm conducted a "social-media scavenger hunt" with clues dribbled out on Twitter and Flicker, the photo-sharing site.

So Young was determined to get one of his agency's biggest clients, Graco, maker of baby products, on Twitter. He was already using Twitter on Graco's behalf, to a degree. But Lindsay Lebresco, Graco's Public-Relations Manager and one of its prominent staff bloggers, initially wasn't convinced Twitter was worth the bother.

She remembers one "dark and stormy night" when she and Young were traveling by road to a gathering of "mommy bloggers" who are among the firm's most passionate clientele. Young, frantically exchanging tweets with those very mothers on his cell phone, seemed oblivious to Lebresco at the wheel.

"I was trying to engage Paull in conversation, and he kept ignoring me," Lebresco said. "He was talking to his mombloggers."

Lebresco finally decided to see what Twitter is all about. Young was eager to show her, though the self-confessed Twitteraholic was unsure how useful it would be to his Graco associate. As he wrote on his blog early this year:[47]

"I don't hide the fact I love the thing, but I was dubious about its potential direct benefit for clients. That was until last week when my client Graco's PR manager Lindsay Lebresco joined Twitter, and over a few days since I've witnessed a bunch of positive results."

---

47 blog.converseon.com/2008/01/17
/examples-of-twitter-providing-business-benefit

The service, as it turned out, is perfect for nurturing relationships with Graco's famously loyal customers, and for giving the firm a human face. Lebresco knows all about that. As one of several workers who post on the company's blog, she is unusually forthcoming about her personal life:[48]

"There is a short time between books and lights out that I spend with my son that is precious to me. My husband takes my daughter to bed and my son and I are left to create magic together. (I'm actually getting teary-eyed writing this because I'm traveling today and know I will miss tonight's ritual.)"

Twitter has become another way for Lebresco, the mother of a toddler and a preschooler, to talk about her parenting adventures as she tries to bond with her clientele. "Graco isn't made up of a bunch of old guys coming out with products," she told me. "It's a company made up of parents. We're going through what other new parents are going through."

On Twitter, she says, she can "tap someone on the shoulder and say, 'Why don't you come over here and follow me? I see you're a mom. I'll bet we'll have a lot in common. And by the way, I work with Graco and have good products.'"

LindsayLebresco: Bad morning drop off at daycare. My son "HATES! school" which makes me sad... What a way to start the day.

LindsayLebresco: check out which celeb blogged for Graco in Honor of Father's Day (hint: Sex and the City!) http://tinyurl.com/4uu6b3

LindsayLebresco: It's snowing in my dining room. Just gave kids powdered sugar donuts for b-fast. Why would I do that??

LindsayLebresco: OK- boss just stopped by to tell me she's 5cm dilated & fully effaced! Yes-she's in the office still!!

---

48 blog.gracobaby.com/lindsay-lebresco

Lebresco says she aspires to be a parent first, and a company spokes-woman second, when she's on Twitter. She had posted to her account hundreds of times when I interviewed her last summer, "And of that, honestly, about 15 are Graco ones related to products," she told me. Graco does not have an @Graco account.

Paull Young, meanwhile, has continued communing with momblog-gers. The man's role at Converseon is that of backup to his client Graco, doing the background scanning of the Twitterverse to see what's being said about the company, and communicating with key Twitter users who show an unusual interest in Graco. He tweets as @paullyoung.

"I have a very diverse collection of people I follow," Young told me. "When we hold an event, I try to get to know all the mombloggers (in the area) so we will know each other before the event...Many of them have become good friends."

Lebresco says, "It's frightening how in touch with this group he is."

The Twitter lesson: It's all about relationships. Make friends among influential folks in the Twitterverse, and business for you and your corporate clientele is certain to follow.

Making Professional Connections

Mark Palony says he is a "social media novice." The marketing manager at SoftBrands, a Minneapolis-based software company, knew virtually nothing about Twitter until hearing about it from his public-re-lations and new-media consultant, Albert Maruggi, earlier this year.

Maruggi, a P.R. veteran, had already spent months dragging his pal Palony into the Web 2.0 era. He had helped SoftBrands publish a blog, create radio-like internet-audio shows called podcasts, and more.

Now Maruggi, a St. Paul public-relations practitioner and a senior fellow at the Society for New Communications Research, wanted Palony to dig deeper into cyberspace, to begin developing relation-ships instead of just parroting information. Twitter is perfect for getting beyond what he calls "brochureware" and interacting with actual humans, Maruggi argues. The social-media evangelist has repeatedly emphasized this on his series of Marketing Edge podcasts, which have drawn a loyal following:[49]

waltcamp45: @AlbertMaruggi Wanted to thank you for continually plugging Twitter on the Marketing Edge—I just joined and am having a blast

Twitter can be a hard sell in business settings, however. "When I start talking Twitter to people at certain companies that shall remain nameless, they think I've lost my marbles," Maruggi told me. "I get lots of puzzled facial expressions. They don't think Twitter is useful at all."

So, before getting into relationship building on Twitter, Maruggi talks about something simpler: keyword searching on Twitter. Using a search engine such as Tweet Scan or the search engine built into Twitter, he has business types key in terms related to their firms and products, as well as those of competitors. This gets their attention, he said, because they invariably pull up plenty of references. They realize that the Twitterverse is talking about them—and that they aren't part of those conversations.

"When I have their attention," Maruggi adds, "I talk to them about the culture of Twitter. I tell them that Twitter isn't about saying you have the greatest thing since sliced bread. It isn't about you selling your stuff. It is about making connections and sharing thoughts."

He likens Twitter interactions to six hours of golf with clients or prospects. Tweeting might cover the same range of topics as chitchat on the links: food, kids, sports and the local traffic. No business deals are being made there, Maruggi said, and that isn't really the point. It's about developing relationships and nurturing friendships:

AlbertMaruggi: "Cheers" and Twitter have plenty in common, society has few "Cheers" in physical world, insert twitter to replace corner bar comfort

---

49 providentpartners.net/blog

This is what Palony learned when dipping into Twitter. He initially had trouble grasping the service's value. But when he did a Tweet Scan search for the acronym "SAP"—his company's software is designed to integrate with software made by German software giant SAP—he pulled up hundreds of relevant tweets. Many of such Twitter references came from within SAP offices located in the United States.

That was crucial for Palony to know because, like all SAP-affiliated "software solution partners," SoftBrands craves closer ties to the SAP mother ship. That can be difficult to accomplish, though, because thousands of such partners exist around the planet, and it's difficult for an obscure Midwestern company to get noticed—at least by normal means.

Twitter helped Palony break through. He was soon following Mike Prosceno, a stateside SAP worker who oversees "social media relations"—which involves tracking anything being said about SAP in the Twitterverse, the blogosphere and elsewhere in cyberspace. "Twitter is an important and powerful tool," Prosceno told me, "though we're still in the early phases of learning its true business capabilities."

Its friendship-building capabilities are already obvious, however. Prosceno and Palony quickly got to know each other on Twitter. Prosceno learned about SoftBrand's podcast efforts and its blog, and he said he "struck up a relationship" that continues to this day.

Palony recalls this budding friendship as "his single best use of Twitter." He wouldn't have felt comfortable ever calling up Prosceno even if he had known about the social-media worker, but "Twitter broke those walls down. I got access."

Palony is now a Twitter believer. "The value for me is making connections with people who have similar interests, personal or professional," he told me. He's a Minnesota Wild professional-hockey fan, for instance, and has exchanges with a San Jose Sharks fanatic:

MarkPalony: @mediaphyter Here's hoping my Wild and your Sharks meet in a later round

mediaphyter: @MarkPalony That's what I'm hoping for, too :)

mediaphyter: @MarkPalony Go Wild! And go Sharks! :)

And over time he has amassed a network of professional acquaintances with whom he is in continual contact, which makes eventual physical meetings easy—"The preliminaries are out of the way because you've already known them for some time," he said.

Maruggi, the public-relations operative who nudged Palony into the Twitterverse, finds the service to be vital in his own work, as well. He said his "boutique" agency operates with a personal touch, meaning he and his second-in-command, Mike Keliher, are on Twitter as individuals (Mike is @mjkeliher) in addition to using their company identity. Most corporate Twitterers should and do take this personal approach, Keliher told me.

Maruggi and Keliher like to have a good time on Twitter. It is fun to "vent, tell jokes, make friends," Keliher recently wrote in a Twitter-for-Business tipsheet for his public-relations peers. He elaborates: "Whether you're Twittering under a company name or your own, being personable is a must. Twitter is opt-in. If you're not interesting and adding value, you're going to have a tough time making friends."

The Twitter lesson: If you're a tiny player in a crowded field, find a way to get noticed. The Twitterverse is one way to bypass traditional channels and make powerful friends.

Nearly Missing the Boat

Page One Public Relations was in crisis late last year because, by its own admission, it was late to the social-media revolution. "We were behind the curve," said Craig Oda, a founder and co-partner at the Silicon Valley-based agency, which places an emphasis on technology-related P.R.

"We were a traditional P.R. firm," he said. "But a lot of our clients wanted us to build online communities." That's what social media, including Twitter, is about. Slower to embrace these new tools, though, Page One lost three major deals. "To be honest, that was a wakeup call," Oda added.

Since then, the agency has placed an internal emphasis on "social media services," with one staffer, Shelly Milam, heading the effort. It has increased its visibility on Twitter, though Oda admits he regarded the service with skepticism at first. "When it came out, we thought it would be one of those fads that would pass. But it is sticking around."

Page One had nearly 30 clients as of this writing, and ten of those were actively using Twitter in their public-relations strategies. These include the Linux Foundation, which promotes the Linux computer operating system, and SourceForge, a software company and computer-code repository that also runs such tech sites as ThinkGeek and Slashdot.

Page One also lured CrowdSPRING, a website that serves as an online marketplace for creative-design projects, onto Twitter. "It's value had to prove itself," Pete Burgeson, the company's Marketing Director, now admits. "I'd say I viewed it with healthy skepticism."

But it has become one more way to connect with potential customers. Burgeson also is addicted to searches for keywords like "logo," since logo design is one emphasis on his site. Looking for that word is one way to connect with people who want to sell their logos on his site, or who are looking for logo designers, he told me.

crowdSPRING: Once you land that perfect company name, check us out for your logo design! http://crowdspring.com

Twitter "is like a big cocktail at the end of the day," he added. "You find people to make conversation. There is value in that conversation. That value is immeasurable."

The Twitter lesson: It is never too late to capitalize on the latest business-building online trend. You just have to be alert enough to recognize its potential and make it your own!

A Giant Embraces Twitter

Matt Dickman, Agency V.P. of Digital Marketing at public-relations giant, Fleishman-Hillard, sees a bit of eye rolling among his P.R. peers when he brings up Twitter. So he grabs their attention by recounting the

Twitterverse response on the evening of August 1, 2007, when a Minneapolis freeway-bridge collapsed, killing 13 people and sending dozens of cars into the Mississippi River.

Dickman says he grasped the power of Twitter shortly after the incident when he began receiving tweets about the incident from average users long before mainstream-media outlets such as CNN were providing reports about it. "The whole story was unfolding right on my phone," he recalled. "The bridge collapse showed the speed" of Twitter, he observed, "the unfiltered nature of conversations. Everyone had access to the same publishing tools."

How is this news event relevant to public-relations agencies and their corporate clients? It's all about that speed, said Dickman.

"Companies can use Twitter (internally) to get information out faster," just as ordinary citizens in Minneapolis did, he argues. This is important within large corporations that have multiple offices around the country or the world. "The old model of dropping an email to the whole company" doesn't work anymore, he said. Twitter is potentially more effective because updates made by anyone within the organization are viewable by all, quickly, on a web page or mobile device.

One of Fleishman-Hillard's clients, an international telecom company that Dickman was not at liberty to identify, uses that very approach. "It uses Twitter as a kind of internal information-sharing system," he said. "People from around the globe can update their accounts, and these are fed out to the rest of the company." They're viewable "in real time" on a customized web page, meaning workers don't even have to use the generic Twitter web interface. Company leaders can even show their geographical locations, which "gives people a sense of the global nature of the company," Dickman added.

Dickman, based in Cleveland and tweeting as @mattdickman, isn't the only Fleishman-Hillard operative using Twitter. The super-agency, with 80 offices around the world, has embraced the service in other ways.

Mark Senak, a Washington, D.C.-based senior vice president focused on health-care public affairs, regards Twitter as a vital information-gathering tool. He's subscribed to the likes of @USAgov, which works as an adjunct to the U.S. government's main web portal, and pushes out a continual series of information updates. Senak, an info-junkie who also subscribes to lots of RSS feeds, devours those tweets. He also likes @NASA.

Senak, who tweets as @eyeonfda because he follows matters related to the Federal Drug Administration, is also an obsessive user of Tweet Scan and other Twitter search engines. These allow him to quickly spot chatter about health- and drug-related issues that might be relevant to his agency's clients in the health-care sphere (he declined to name any clients).

eyeonfda: FDA approves genetic test that determines if breast cancer patients are good candidates for Herceptin

eyeonfda: FDA Extends Review Period for Daiichi Sankyo, Lilly Investigative Antiplatelet Drug, Prasugrel

Mobile Twitter use is a godsend, Senak said. "I can take my cell phone up on the Hill for congressional hearings and tweet about testimony as it happens."

Kendra Bracken, a Fleishman-Hillard vice president focused on consumer-centric "digital brands and initiatives," recently guided the AT&T telecommunications titan onto Twitter.

The emphasis was on music—AT&T spent a summer webcasting from several big music festivals, such as the famed Lollapalooza in Chicago, and the Bonnaroo Music and Arts Festival in rural Tennessee. The company, which offers a variety of music features on its mobile handsets, promoted itself and the concerts via an AT&T Blue Room website and a companion @ATTblueroom identity on Twitter. (It also fashioned a Twitter account for communication with the media, which are increasingly using the service.)

"When we launched the public Twitter channel, we had someone on the ground doing live tweets" from Bonnaroo, and "a team in the office looking at different music blogs and tweeting anything, everything, that was happening," Bracken said. "If there was a celebrity sighting backstage, we tweeted it. We'd literally tweet every 15 minutes or so."

ATTblueroom: We're hearing—though not confirmed—that the Olsen twins are pulling up backstage...

ATTblueroom: We passed the Olsen twins in VIP last night!

It's important to "be committed on Twitter," she said. "You have to keep it up regularly."

The Twitter lesson: In a big public-relations agency, the Twitterverse can have many uses. It can be used internally, or externally on clients' behalf. Use your imagination!

Personal and Professional

On Twitter, the personal and professional often blend. Christine Perkett, founder of the Massachusetts-based P.R. agency, PerkettPR, has discovered this first hand. Her agency is unusually Twitter-active across its ten-state network, which has generated wide-ranging conversations and led to a few surprises.

Twitter users tend to hug when they meet for the first time in person, she's discovered.

"After you have established a relationship and talked for months and months, you feel like you know the person," Perkett told me. "I know it's corny. My husband doesn't get it. As an engineer he understands the value of Twitter, but he does not feel the need to build relationships. He thinks, 'Why talk with all these strangers?' He does follow me on Twitter to see who I'm talking to."

As of this writing, the hubby had yet to tweet using his personal account. Perkett and her husband did team up on a blog[50] and a related Twitter account focused on their training for a Marathon in Dublin, Ireland. They happened to draw most of their blog followers from Twitter, Perkett said. "We built a great community of people eager to share advice and opinions on running gear and techniques."

---

50 www.training4dublin.com

training4dublin: We are a big mess of injuries—already! Funny, most have nothing to do with running.

training4dublin: Just an FYI ... eating a 1 pound hot dog prior to running turns out to actually *not* be a good idea.

In her public-relations work, meanwhile, Perkett said she has encountered a great deal of skepticism about Twitter. When recently speaking to professional peers at a conference, she brought up social media and "the majority of faces in the room looked at us like we were crazy," she wrote on the Perkett blog.[51]

She argues, though, that Twitter is essential in the public-relations agency for building a network of "frenemies," P.R. practitioners who compete yet can compare notes on their accomplishments and commiserate over similar struggles:[52]

Through Twitter, we've had the opportunity to build relationships like never before—not only with other P.R. and social media professionals, but reporters, bloggers, analysts and others in relevant—and sometimes not-at-all-relevant—industries.

Perkett admitted she needed a bit of persuading to try Twitter in the first place. Her just-hired director of social media "convinced me to get onto it and play around with it" last year, she recalled. "As president, I wanted to test it out first to make sure it was a useful tool for us. We should adopt technology from the top down. It's not just my employees. I have to make sure I'm participating, too." She now tweets as @missusP and contributes to a @PerkettPR account.

missusP: Had two great client conversations today about the value of social media. Turned one vehement NO around & another to "okay, tell me more..."

---

51 perkettprsuasion.com/2008/05/09
/drop-the-excuses-and-start-participating
52 perkettprsuasion.com/2008/01/22
/how-twitter-can-expand-your-world-frenemies-and-all

missusP: I don't care who you are, if you have 2k followers and only follow 1 it makes it hard to believe you are conversing rather than spouting.

As of this writing, PerkettPR boasted more than two dozen staff or company Twitter accounts, which is quite a large number considering the agency employed about 35 people. She counted several Twitter-enthused companies among her clients, as well.

One of these, Boston-based Mzinga, is a Twitter natural because it builds its own social networks for major websites, such as those of ABC News and ESPN. Mzinga-powered features on those sites enable live chat, forum discussions and blogging. Is it any wonder Aaron Strout, who until October was the company's Vice President of New Media, groks Twitter?

Strout recently conducted a company-hiring experiment, vetting applicants for a pair of jobs using Twitter and other social networks while banning resumes and other standard job-hunting tactics. He eventually hired a woman for one of the jobs after she contacted him via Twitter, Facebook and LinkedIn (and met at a gathering of Boston-area social-media types).

Like Perkett, Strout uses Twitter to nurture his personal relationships. He tweets about the Red Sox with other fans, and used to gather Twitter friends for intimate barbecues outside Mzinga headquarters, where he'd set up picnic tables. "It's just five or 10 people" each time, including the likes of @pistachio (Boston-area business coach and famed Twitter evangelist Laura Fitton), he told me last summer.

Strout left Mzinga in October to become head of marketing at social-commerce firm Powered.com, but vowed to remain active in the Twitterverse.

The Twitter lesson: Don't think about the Twitterverse as just for work or just for fun. It often can be both. Don't fear this. Embrace that blurring of personal and professional!

Tweeting About Cancer

Almost anything is up for discussion on Twitter, even cervical cancer. A keyword search for that phrase turns up lots of hits.

No wonder Lippe Taylor Inc., a New York City-based advertising, marketing and public-relations agency, has embraced the service. Lippe focuses mainly on consumer brands for women. Such brands include Digene, maker of a test to detect the human papillomavirus (or HPV) that is a precursor to cervical cancer.

That's why James Gregson, Director of Emerging Media at Lippe, is continually searching for chatter about cancer on Twitter. He's looking for cancer patients and cancer survivors to help spread the word that women should routinely request an HPV test along with a Pap smear after the age of 30.

Gregson said he was initially skeptical about Twitter when he heard about it late last year. "I was thinking, 'This is so strange.'"

But he soon realized Twitter was a part of a global conversation he needed to join. "It's no longer just blogs and web forums," he said. "It's also social networks." Along with Twitter, he now routinely scours MySpace, Facebook and social-bookmarking sites like Yahoo-owned Delicious. "It's a P.R. person's dream to have all of these various social-media sites where people are talking about your topic of interest."

The Twitter lesson: You never know what will come up in the Twitter-verse. Much of it is wacky and inane, but some tweets will touch on the most profound subjects imaginable.

An Agency Gets Mysterious

Sterling Cross Communications in Maple Grove, Minnesota, tried something a bit offbeat on Twitter earlier this year: it created a mysterious @motoi2go identity that described itself only as "a fresh and amazing cultural experience about to arrive in the Twin Cities. Stay tuned for more!"

This Twitter-based promotion, on behalf of moto-i, a Japanese-themed eatery and sake microbrewery, was intended to pump up interest in the establishment amid stiff competition in the restaurant-rich Twin Cities. The Twitter-based P.R. campaign, conducted over several months, played coy at first as the establishment's owners remained secretive about their unusual establishment. As the late-October opening day approached, though, it began trumpeting itself as "the first sake micro-brewery outside of Japan."

This campaign was an unusual Twitter approach with only moderate success—@motoi2go drew some 200 followers—but Sterling Cross gets points for creative thinking.

The small firm, founded by the husband-and-wife team of Mary and Chris Lower, has placed a heavy emphasis on social and "viral" media. Old public-relations approaches, via traditional pitches to print publications and broadcast companies, are increasingly ineffective, Chris told me last summer. "The old messages are not working," he said. "Telemarketing is getting crushed. Direct mail is not succeeding."

"So about a year and half ago, we began moving everything to the internet," Chris said.

The Lowers became Twitterers—he is @MrChristopherL and she tweets as @PRMoxie—who advertised their handles prominently on their agency's website. They're also the ones who tweeted together as @motoi2go. "We are trying to build up buzz," Chris said.

Reaction to this approach wasn't all positive. Erica Mauter of Minneapolis Metblogs tweeted in early autumn:

swirlspice: @motoi2go So, you're going to have some actual news in the very near future, right? Because I'm getting bored.

In the Twitter exchange that followed, Sterling Cross had to apologize for construction-permit delays that slowed work on the restaurant and sapped the Twitter campaign of some suspense and specificity. With moto-i finally launched, though, Sterling Cross planned to use the eatery's Twitter identity to announce events, specials and new sake batches from the gleaming back-room brewery, Chris Lower told me over a moto-i meal.

Sterling Cross has found Twitter to be useful in other ways. Creative-media director Scott Baird (@mediapirate) uses it to hire contractors for print and web-based projects. Twitter is "an ideal talent pool," he said, allowing him to "establish relationships with contractors prior to our working together."

Baird also anticipates finding new clients for his agency through Twitter, which lets him tap into an extensive web of contacts. "The power of Twitter is the relationships," he told me. "It's an element built by time and constant interaction."

Chris Lower, meanwhile, uses Twitter to relentlessly promote his various clients—but in a way that's useful instead of irksome. If a client is appearing on a TV show, for instance, he'll tweet that fact so his followers can tune in.

The Twitter lesson: When tapping into the Twitterverse for public-relations purposes, use your imagination and try something new. Twitter is good for basic business stuff, too.

What Would You Do For...

"What would you do for a Klondike Bar?" The Golin Harris P.R. Agency recently posed this familiar question in the form of a video contest[53] on behalf of Unilever, the company responsible for such delicacies as Klondike and Dove ice cream bars along with Bryer's ice cream.

Along with traditional advertising, handled by an ad agency, the Klondike campaign had a social-media strategy intended to create online excitement. "We had this social-media cake we are trying to bake, with lots of different little pieces going into the recipe," said Rick Wion, a Chicago-based Golin Harris Vice President of Social Media. This included creating YouTube videos, approaching hundreds of blogs for Klondike plugs, and more.

---

53 klondikecontest.com/Home.aspx

Chapter 4: Twitter and Public Relations

Twitter "is just another ingredient in the cake," Wion said. His agency had found plenty of Klondike mentions in the Twitterverse when it ran keyword searches—so it sought to join that conversation by creating a @Klondikebear account ostensibly run by Klondie, a furry, red-scarf-wearing denizen of the Arctic.

"We realized Twitter was by no means the largest or most active social-media space out there," Wion said. "But with a little bit of planning and not too much effort, we added a new component to this program. We found a good voice for the Klondike bear. He's fun, irreverent. He's a hipster."

Klondikebear: I scream, you scream, we all scream for ice cream! All together now....

Klondikebear: Got a call from my agent. I may have a photo shoot at Klondike HQ in a few weeks. They better fly me 1st class—that's all I'm saying.

How would Twitter users react? Wion admits he feared a bit of a backlash from followers accustomed to real-life interactions who might be resentful of such a boldly commercial incursion. He had encountered little such blowback as of this writing.

The Twitter lesson: Who says a user has to be human, or even real? Why not a fictional, scarf-wearing bear, or some other such? Hey, that's the playful Twitterverse for you.

5 Twitter Veterans Speak Out

Some of the smartest and web-savviest people I know are associated with Social Media Breakfast Twin Cities, a monthly gathering of social-media practitioners and observers in Minnesota.

The drill is a now-familiar one: We all gather in a room and dissect a subject of mutual interest while sipping strong java and munching on something tasty. (Mmm…bacon…) Similar gatherings occur around the country, in a movement pioneered by social-media expert Bryan Person.

So when mapping out this book in my head, I knew I wanted my esteemed local Social Media Breakfast franchise to be involved in some way. I hit on the notion of having the group write one of my book chapters, in the form of Twitter-based discussion about the book's subject matter. I'd coordinate the discussion using my book-related @twitinbiz identity as well as my personal @jojeda identity, and later compile all the tweets here.

I introduced the idea to the group, also known as SMBMSP, in a series of blog posts on the group's site.[54]

During the discussion, I posed a couple of questions to get the conversation flowing. On the first day, I asked:

twitinbiz: Twitter comes up at a party. "More companies should be on it," you say. Crickets. Everyone thinks you're insane. What do you say?

On the second day, I asked:

twitinbiz: Good morning! Today's question: You're starting company. What's your killer Twitter strategy? How will the service help you soar?

I initially intended the discussion to take place over a week, culminating with a physical SMBMSP gathering. I cut off the discussion after only two days, however, as more than enough tweets for a chapter flooded in during that short period.

twitinbiz: In order to get full transcript in book as promised, I'll stop now (I have tons). Let's still do live @smbmsp chat on Friday. Thx

GraemeThickins: got a kick when @jojeda told me he was buried in tweets by Tues for his planned weeklong acceptance of 'em for his book chapter!

The discussion achieved a high profile in the Twitterverse and drew participants beyond Minnesota's borders. Notable ones included Comcast's Frank Eliason, featured in Chapter One, and Veronica McGregor, who is responsible for the highly popular @MarsPhoenix account associated with NASA's Mars Phoenix lander.

jojeda: Just caught on to the fact that @VeronicaMcG (yes, the famed @MarsPhoenix) chimed in today. So did @comcastcares. Honored, happy

What follows is a transcript of the Twitter-based discussion, with only minor editing. It is also viewable online in its complete, unedited form.

---

54 smbmsp.ning.com/profiles/blog/list?user=2f6mbu7xjh86t

I resisted the temptation to tidy up this stream of tweets here, or to mold it into some kind of traditional narrative. That would defeat the purpose of showing you what Twitter looks and feels like.

So, here are a few tips as you dip in. The below is printed in reverse-chronological order with the most recent material higher, like the rest of Twitter. It should therefore make the most sense to you when digested from back to front and not front to back.

Not every tweet will interest you. Those who navigate Twitter encounter a lot of "noise" as they search for a "signal," so just skim along for tweets that appear compelling while skipping over the rest.

Note that some tweets are responses to other tweets appearing earlier and further down in the Twitter stream. You will know this if the responding posting is prefaced with the "@" symbol followed by the username of another user. Following such conversation threads may be a bit tricky, but that is part of the fun.

Relax, enjoy, and learn a thing or two from a bunch of bright minds.

jojeda: Thanks to all at @smbmsp and #smbmsp and for your interest in (and support for) my http://twitin.biz project. I had fun today :-)

swirlspice: @jojeda is so delightfully nerdy. Love this guy. He's up front with his Captain Janeway mug talking about his book.

GraemeThickins: got a kick when @jojeda told me he was buried in tweets by Tues for his planned weeklong acceptance of 'em for his book chapter!

BigYapper: @jojeda @twitinbiz Assume you saw this from Chris Brogan (50 Ideas on using Twitter for Business)—but just in case; http://twurl.nl/j7bua0

justacoolcat: @jojeda Is your book going to mention spam and the use of porno girls?

hgeorge: So sad I could not participate in today I had some ideas but was busy in faculty presentations. Oh wait, educate=first step. yup!

Philson: @twitinbiz first step would need to be educate customers about Twitter. 95% have never heard of it.

jojeda: @smbmsp All done. If we keep going, I can't get all tweets into http://twitin.biz. I'd still like to have chat at @smbmsp Friday.

smbmsp: @jojeda You're done then? Glad we could all participate. Anything else we #smbmsp-ers can do?

twitinbiz: In order to get full transcript in book as promised, I'll stop now (I have tons). Let's still do live @smbmsp chat on Friday. Thx

KiraMo: @twitinbiz In other words, use twitter to tease.

KiraMo: @twitinbiz I would use Twitter as a reference to blog posts, and drive traffic back to the company's main website with more meaty content

AaronWeiche: @jojeda—I would focus on how to get my target market ON Twitter, then I could use the tool on many levels. Must create audience

cullect: @jojeda I a point of following existing and potential customers. Twitter is also @cullect's primary cust. support channel

navaja1cortes: @twitinbiz—I would have a really cool background, prof pic, and even add it to emailemail signatures. You should also have a creative name.

parsifal: @jojeda For a news organization, I think Twitter's a great way to break important news (not too often!).

parsifal: @jojeda If you made software, you could advertise advanced features and tips.

johnreilly: @jojeda We love GetSatisfaction.com at @trms. It helps us take action on tweets, turning them into full-fledged customer support.

PussycatDoll: @dougpollei makes excellent point—companies could start by being good listeners. Let customers help you build strategy/content.

andyburns: @jojeda Follow @Reuters to find out top news... (I'm a shill).

twitinbiz: To elaborate on my earlier question today, what creative stuff would you do with Twitter at your new company to really stand out?

PussycatDoll: A good first step may actually be to set up your account and then simply ask a question "What would you like to hear from us"?

PussycatDoll: ... find out what your customers/clients want and/or need from Twitter (or other service) and then give it to them...

PussycatDoll: @trms asks good question. How would you as customer like businesses to use Twitter? What provides value as follower?—discuss.

johnreilly: weird, my last post didn't seem to make it into summize..err.. twitter search. maybe twitter thought it was a bad idea? :)

JDubb: @jojeda I would incorporate Twitter into my customer support strategy.

trms: Enjoying the "using Twitter in business" discussion going on with @twitinbiz. How would *you* like us to use Twitter?

patrickrhone: @jojeda Set up an account, staff it 24/7 with someone who is Twitter savvy at all times and let it help drive my cust. service.

mjkeliher: Anyone interested in commenting on the usefulness of Twitter in business communication, check this out: http://is.gd/1K4d

swirlspice: @twitinbiz Most important thing is a human voice must be evident. Not just feed dumping. I'd offer Twitter-only specials.

dougpollei: @twitinbiz many companies are good at following others and broadcasting their message but not listening and responding. Twitspam.

smbmsp: Remember to use hashtag when answering this question: http://twitter.com/twitinbiz/statuses/892117133

twitinbiz: Good morning! Today's question: You're starting company. What's your killer Twitter strategy? How will the service help you soar?

rout1000: After taking care of the internal as @jonmierow said, solidify your identity and then it's off to make friends with the world.

rickmahn: Expanding on @nathaneide: Listen to ascertain context, then participate when it will bring value. It may/may not pertain to you.

rickmahn: Twitter is a great component of personal branding strategy. Not only for what I say, but for word of mouth referrals as well.

bigboxcar: @jojeda DO NOT just set up a profile and then follow every Twitterer you can click on! This is not Direct Mail marketing.

nathaneide:—Listen, listen, listen, then talk.

jpavleck: @jojeda easy. astro-turfers. people that 'complain' on twitter, we respond fast back and 'fix' it. people think we care—easy

jonmierow: internal communication first. make sure those inside the company know how to use it. then marketing, PR & customer service

pfhyper: Netflix should definitely be monitoring Twitter. We'll see if my tweets get any results. (see prev.)

jojeda: Just caught on to the fact that @VeronicaMcG (yes, the famed @MarsPhoenix) chimed in today. So did @comcastcares. Honored, happy

jojeda: Already mulling which guayabera to wear for the live climax of at Friday's @smbmsp. Decisions, decisions...

twitinbiz: Posted to the @smbmsp blog: "Twitter Book: Pat yourselves on the back!" http://xrl.us/twitinbizstats

rickmahn: @jojeda Kudos on the great response to your Twitter-Book project

rickmahn: Ah, I just made it home. I hope to see what's been happening with @jojeda & @twitinbiz

C3POJones: A personal success story for Twitter. Got great ideas for a ministry speaking engagement from twitter connection @AarontWhite.

AaronWeiche: Besides new contacts & collab projects, we have had increased interest in our CMS tool from other web shops. Product awareness.

twitinbiz: Terrific discussion today, fellow tweeps. Ready for round two? I'll post another question in the AM. http://xrl.us/twitinbizchat

jojeda: Terrific discussion today, fellow tweeps. Ready for round two? I'll post another question in the AM. http://xrl.us/twitinbizchat

PussycatDoll: @nathaneide Very—if you can't connect the two :)

nathaneide: @PussycatDoll—In this age, how separate are the personal from the professional?

PussycatDoll: @bigboxcar At times when appropriate will compose post on personal account then just copy & paste on pro account (using Twhirl).

PussycatDoll: @mnheadhunter That's why Tweetdeck and Twhirl are so helpful, manage (tw) and organize (td) multiple info from single screens.

MNHeadhunter: @PussycatDoll Separate accounts I don't know. I have seen (and experienced) getting business because of people getting to know me

PussycatDoll: @bigboxcar personal—don't see the need for my clients/employer to see/hear my personal opinions on many subjects.

Scottpete: Twitter provides insight on what your customers are saying... to each other. In how many ways could you put that insight to use??

PussycatDoll: ...can't wait for inevitable stories about how co's couldn't land (or keep) client(s) because of exec's personal tweet(s).

bigboxcar: re: don't use single Twitter account... Had not heard before. So is @PussycatDoll your personal account, or professional account?

PussycatDoll: ....once your thoughts, responses, jokes, pics, etc are posted (assuming you're not private) they're there forever. Too much info

PussycatDoll: I'll say this one last time; using a single Twitter account for both your personal and professional is a HUGE mistake......

Philson: @mholterhaus Which is exactly the problem w/SM & Twitter adoption by biz. Wall st. doesn't allow time for much patience.

PussycatDoll: Smart co's will take their time to determine why/when/how they'll pursue a social media strategy that may/may not include Twitter

mholterhaus: it seems most naysayers haven't used twitter long enough to experience its many marvels—social media takes micro-patience

bigboxcar: @PussycatDoll Ironic that @twitter doesn't handle customer service well via twitter! My personal ex: http://is.gd/1HXU

nathaneide: @PussycatDoll Agreed. It's all about setting and meeting expectations.

PussycatDoll: Once you give customers/others the impression that you'll respond to them via Twitter you better be prepared to respond.. forever

MNHeadhunter: Early adopters tend to know other cool people who know many others, a useful networking tool to source and recruit for companies

PussycatDoll: I think that people sometimes forget to answer this essential question; "Just because we can, does it mean we should?"

Philson: @mikerynchek Sure but Zappos has a bit of a cult status. Would the same impact be felt by Famous Footwear or even Kmart?

MNHeadhunter: The ability for small companies to compete with the big boys on a level playing field in marketing and PR

perfectporridge: @myklroventine I found out about MSP bridge collapse via Twitter, and Edwards' affair, George Carlin's death, Miley's topless pix

jojeda: @perfectporridge @DeRushaL Mr. DeRusha is the only reason I would even think to watching local news on occasion. He's a big draw.

jojeda: @PussycatDoll I understand Comcast continually expands the staff working under @comcastcares (Frank Eliason), now at dozen or so.

PussycatDoll: ...if "engaging" is what you're after, then get ready to hire multiple bodies for new position—Bitchfest Monitor

myklroventine: @Philson We're on to "If Twitter was a tree, what kind of tree would it be?"

PussycatDoll: ...let's see what happens to @comcastcares et al when more than .001% of their customers discover Twitter....

Philson: Just hopped on...where did the discussion leave off? Still answering the Twitter at a party question?

PussycatDoll: The idea that large companies can "engage" an audience via Twitter or other once the platform hits critical mass is laughable...

navaja1cortes: I just read @twitinbiz's post about why companies should/shouldn't have a Twitter...very interesting and will give my 2 cents in a bit :-)

Scottpete: To be customer-centric, you need to be where your customers are—hear the buzz. Do your customers use Twitter? How do you know?

nathaneide: re @VeronicaMcG—"Any company that sees the value of "word of mouth" needs to be on Twitter. Twitter = global word of mouth."

myklroventine: @VeronicaMcG Well said. Comparing Twitter to WOM is a great way to help biz wrap their arms around the concept.

perfectporridge: @DeRushaJ Getting to know you via Twitter is the only reason I ever tune into local news. And I still want you to mow my lawn.

nathaneide: @perfectporridge, @DeRushaJ,—Interesting. I have actually changed my online news habits thanks to reporters/outlets who tweet

newcoventry: there is also a lot to be said about customer service triage via twitter. constant monitoring and fast action. like @comcastcares

MrChristopherL: @veronicamcg—In theory that would b great, but blasting your news on Twitter is no better than any other blasting of a release

DeRushaJ: @jojeda And that human side of me has completely repulsed "professionals" like @perfectporridge

perfectporridge: @jojeda As a PR professional, Twitter offers a unique window into the human side of reporters, what actually interests them, etc.

VeronicaMcG: @jojeda Old biz model: issue news via PR Newswire and hope media run your story. New biz model: issue news yourself via Twitter.

rickmahn: Interestingly, it's the GenXer's that seem to realize and enable the business aspects of Twitter.

MrChristopherL:—ours are in Twitter, just a preference of the data collection tool! ;)

MrChristopherL:—@jojeda—the younglings think we are ridiculous for twittering instead of texting, yet their followers are all in their phone

nathaneide: Twitter allows them to hear the customer much more economically than playing phone tag, reading RFPs and hitting the tradeshows

nathaneide: Too often sales expects marketing to get them the leads, then take over with whatever "pitch" it is they use over and over.

jojeda: @jamuraa I don't rely solely on Twitter for news, but it works well in tandem with RSS, Alltop and manual peeks at NYT-ish sites.

jojeda: @CamGross This is true, though I've found that college students aren't Twitter-aware to the degree that slightly older nerds are.

byteCoder: Twitter is noise. Sometimes the most interesting items are found in the fringes of the noise band. Twitter enables this discovery.

nathaneide:—If sales wants to be active in the market and truly know what the customer wants, they need to use all tools in their arsenal

jamuraa: I use twitter now as almost my only breaking news source, and it works well if the news isn't so big that it causes failwhale

CamGross: Consumers under 25 are immersed in this world more than in mass media. They will expect (or maybe demand) this kind of contact

pure_drivel: Twitter has also been particularly helpful in establishing connections between journalists/webcomic artists and their customers.

comcastcares: @CamGross And a company should admit fess up.

CamGross: @comcastcares SM consumers would prefer to hear a company admit to a fault/flaw rather then hearing the "all is rosy" PR message

nathaneide: Great discussion on Twitter in Business for @jojeda's book. Follow along http://tinyurl.com/5nd7lh

twitinbiz: Hey, cool, #twitinbiz is listed in Twitter Search (formerly Summize) trending topics.

nathaneide: Need to get sales on Twitter, not just marketing. Alas, our target audience is slow to adopt any new tech, and blocks most apps.

myklroventine: @jojeda Great example. One that will be repeated more & more: Tim Russert's death, Chinese earthquake, even I-35 bridge collapse.

jojeda: @perfectporridge Agreed, no other online service has helped me connect with friendly and fabulous people the way Twitter has. has

jojeda: @pure_drivel It's pretty wild/cool when you gripe about Comcast on Twitter and @comcastcares phones you literally minutes later:)

jojeda: @myklroventine I'll always remember how Twitter (Summize trending topics) was how I heard about the release of Ingrid Betancourt.

jojeda: @CamGross At one firm in my book that shall remain nameless, PR blocked my interview efforts so I just DM-ed the main Twitter guy

myklroventine: @CamGross Exactly! My biz convos re: needing 2 B on Twitter are much like convos 10 years ago re: why need 2 have a website.

CamGross: I suspect a major barrier for engaging on Twitter is the fear of "what employees might say" because the message isn't PR scrubbed

blamedesign: @jojeda Your company is already being promoted/trashed/whatever on Twitter right now. You just need to join the conversation.

byteCoder: Reducing your thoughts to their pithy core, rough elements is up to you. Are your sound bites content-full or content-free?

CamGross: not wanting to engage on Twitter reminds me of companies in the early 90s that didn't want to have a website for fear of hacking.

myklroventine: @slolee Not me. Filling up on cookies and coffee. Ready for more.

slolee: I think all the Twitters went to lunch :)

hjortur: @jojeda People are going to talk about your company, whether you participate or not. Are you going to have a say?

myklroventine: @rickmahn Great point esp. w/ Twitter scooping major news outlets on stories like earthquakes and world events

rickmahn: A company's ability to quickly respond to realtime feedback and issues or an outage or natural disaster are possible as well.

myklroventine: Just found out there are cookies in our office kitchen. Who needs a better biz reason than that for Twitter?

rickmahn: Looks like in the Top 10 search results... http://twitter.com/twitgeistr/statuses/891253731

myklroventine: Some tweets getting dropped from Twitscoop, seems like summize/search.twitter doing a slightly better job http://is.gd/1HGv

twitgeistr: Top 10 words right now: work, find, other, twitinbiz, times, cool, morning, feel, someone, google. See http://tinyurl.com/2jzqq2

MrChristopherL: Twitter facilitated a quicker immersion/adaption to texting for our boomer clients...

donmball: Twitter = A low-cost way to rectify customer service deficiencies as @comcastcares is doing.

donmball: Twitter = Low cost method of reaching out to sneezers as @wholefoods is doing.

myklroventine: @newcoventry Yes! Zappos is great example because of the commitment as a whole company too. Seen this? http://is.gd/bGl

rickmahn: Similar to a face2face conversation, Twitter "tweets" require being read in order to formulate an intelligent response.

byteCoder: The party conversation is like Twitter, except with a smaller number of participants. Are party conversations insane?

MrChristopherL: Twitter is best when used in conjunction with other tools, and when combined with the next step ie: real life mtgs, etc

newcoventry: @jojeda Zappos is a very strong example of how companies can benefit from twitter. Real people, fervent devotion to the brand

planetrussell: Those of us interested in Twitter for business can follow Twitscoop's conversation at http://tinyurl.com/62wvno

hgeorge: Like the reality show phenom, people like getting an inside view. Twitter can provide a biz with some desirable transparency

myklroventine: @slolee @nathaneide @MrChristopherL The ones who truly engage & participate will stand out & win. Darwinian social networking :)

donmball: Twitter = the world's cheapest market research tool.

myklroventine: More on @wholefoods: taking good advantage of what is essentially and opt -in fan base

slolee: @nathaneide @MrChristopherL but if companies reach "critical mass" on Twitter, who is still standing out?

myklroventine: Anyone mentioned @wholefoods yet? Great use of Twtr. Human voice, links 2 other branded SM (like flickr), shares pertinent info

taulpaul: I wonder if this is a small sense of omnipresence. God just has bigger ears, and better filters than Twitter.

pure_drivel: @comcastcares You should jump into the conversation if you can—I don't know if Comcast would be cool with that.

nathaneide: @MrChristopherL I think this is a great point. More and more bleeding-edge companies are looking for ways to stand out.

MrChristopherL: We've also been able to utilize Twitter to test messages and other items—sort of an informal focus group...

MrChristopherL: Twitter has allowed for us to create buzz and excitement/awareness in advance of product launch or press release for clients

nathaneide: With the 1 to 1 marketing of today, tools like Twitter can work with your SEM and email strategies and appear less "marketing"

myklroventine: It's also really easy 2 quickly tell if a biz is truly interacting. Just look 4 @replies on their profile. Hard 2 fake engagement

nathaneide: True interaction leads to brand loyalty, and we all know how much more profitable it is to keep a customer than create new ones

pure_drivel: I would immediately point to @comcastcares. Honestly, he's the most helpful customer service rep I've ever seen from the company.

nathaneide: That's a great point @rickmahn. It's true interaction between a corporation and its customers/prospects.

amandam: i've noticed that twitterers often give a heads up of an upcoming negative review which can be mitigated via twitter

johnreilly: @jojeda interacting with customers is energizing; encourages me to keep making products to help them kick ass. (thx @KathySierra)

rickmahn: Because Twitter responses can't be automated, it lends an opportunity for a company to really interact with customers or clients.

myklroventine: Twitter = low initial investment & potential of tremendous return 4 biz. It's a cornerstone of most of my client SM strategies.

pfhyper: @patiomancer Hmm. Your last twitinbiz post showed up.

leeodden: Twitter has helped me plan a NYC vac, connect with new real-world biz friends locally/abroad & is a top 5 referrer to our blog

perfectporridge: Twitter has made me more in-real-life friends than all social networks combined. It's the move valuable networking tool I use

CamGross: Engaging in conversation about your business is better than allowing it to go on behind your back.

johnreilly: @jojeda twitter makes it easy to whine, and no one sends in "customer satisfaction surveys" anymore. savvy companies will adapt.

CamGross: Twitter used well gives a human persona to the company.

patiomancer: My posts about @graywolfpress aren't showing up on Summize. :-/

pure_drivel: If you tweet like an individual, and not a company, Twitter can be a good way to put a more personal face on daily operations.

jojeda: @pfhyper I can feel the rush of air through my hair right now :-)

jojeda: @pfhyper Excellent point!; DM the bios in Twitter style; bios should include full name along with quickie info about what you do.

pfhyper: Wishing I had more time to follow the stream today. Great idea, Julio.

pfhyper: (Please note the TWOOSH.)

pfhyper: Still early-adopter land but us adopters do influence friends and family so business will benefit from Twitter experiments today.

pfhyper: Twemes is broken. Follow at Summize (oops, mean Twitter Search) http://snurl.com/3hf8y

myklroventine: @jamuraa Agreed. Even a brief back and forth w/ co rep is invaluable & could be the diff btwn losing customer & gaining booster.

jojeda: @minnpostnow Mock crab. Do I look like I'm made of money? ;-)

minnpostnow: @jojeda Say, this dip is delicious! Is it crab?

JDubb: @jojeda Twitter is a great tool in the right hands.

twitinbiz: More questions to follow, one each morning through Thursday (culminating with live chat at @smbmsp Friday. Tag your answers with: #twitinbiz

twitinbiz: Help me write a Twitter-book chapter. Background here: http://xrl.us/twitinbizchat. First question here: http://xrl.us/twitinbiz1

rout1000: High return on investment. Last I checked companies like free stuff as much as "teens looking to hookup."

jamuraa: @myklroventine the reason I like companies' reps on here and not political candidates is that the conversation is often 2-way.

taulpaul: @jojeda Your company isn't ready for this type of interaction. When you can tell me what your SOV online is, then we'll talk.

myklroventine: I think Twitter is just as, if not more, useful for listening to customers than sharing info w/ them. That's why biz should use.

bigboxcar: @jojeda Are we supposed to keep our answers to one 140 character response? Just checking.

bigboxcar: jojeda If a company discovers a dialogue about them on twitter (good or bad), it presents a GREAT opportunity to connect to users

bigboxcar: @jojeda ... After you search, then grab me another Summit from the cooler. Great party!

johnreilly: @jojeda twitterers are still "early adopters". if you can appease them, they'll sing your praises loudly and frequently.

johnreilly: @jojeda phone support is painful. for everyone. conversing via tweet is just as engaging, and less time consuming for all.

johnreilly: @jojeda if you can engage with your customers on a more human level, they'll stop thinking of you as faceless corporate evil. :)

windowseat: @jojeda Give specific examples of cool interactions with companies on twitter like @zappos, @wholefoods, @firefox_answers, etc.

MegCanada: You can make connections with your power users, create a human face for your business and troubleshoot user perception.

hgeorge: Being on Twitter gives a more human "face" to a biz, people are less likely to direct negativity toward a person than a business

MegCanada: Twitter can be work-related networking and conversation. If you aren't part of it, you are missing a valuable opportunity.

swirlspice: "Twitter gives a company a chance to respond to its customers on a personal level, with a human voice."

hgeorge: businesses being ON Twitter: plz don't release 4 tweets at one time once a day, and plz follow your followers so they can DM you.

slolee: Also, consumers search their own networks, like Twitter, for info on a company. Why not already be there for them?

slolee: A company on Twitter, even a big corporation like Comcast, can seem more approachable, and create a genuine voice.

rickmahn: Show how quickly the company can address a customer question, complaint or issue by direct interaction.

mjkeliher: Then, I'd explain if you want to know when people are happy or upset with your co., monitoring Twitter is a great place to start.

C3POJones: @jojeda I share success stories. My wife (@slolee) has made multiple advancements for her company through twitter.

benhedrington: @jojeda Otherwise people think you are spewing buzzwords... http://bit.ly/viz-socal-conversation

nathaneide: I show the integration between twitter, facebook and various company websites, talking about number of touches and branding.

benhedrington: @jojeda You must show them the value, visualize the conversation. This is why I created 'spy' http://spy.appspot.com

rickmahn: Pull out my phone and demonstrate how Twitter works through SMS.

jojeda: First question: Twitter comes up at a party. "More companies should be on it," you say. Everyone thinks you're nuts. What do you say? #twitinbiz

jojeda: Help me write a Twitter-book chapter. Background here: http://xrl.us/twitinbizchat. First question here: http://xrl.us/twitinbiz1

jojeda: To those helping to write a chapter in my Twitter book today, please tag your tweets with hashtag #twitinbiz. Thanks.

myklroventine: @jojeda Looking forward to it!

twitinbiz: Help write a chapter in a book about Twitter, beginning tomorrow. All are welcome. http://xrl.us/twitinbizchat Book deets: http://twitin.biz

twitinbiz: @smbmsp @rickmahn Twitter book: are we ready to rock? Y'all get to write a chapter this week, starting tomorrow. http://xrl.us

twitinbiz: Twitter book: Are we ready to rock? http://tinyurl.com/66qfzf

twitinbiz: Twitter book: Kicking off the discussion: http://tinyurl.com/6xnsp4

6 Twitter Tips, Tricks and Tools

Twitter is utter simplicity. This is what makes it so appealing for web-savvy companies, which can start promoting themselves and meeting their clientele with little effort. There is virtually no learning curve!

At the same time, Twitter's popularity during the past two years has spawned an intricate ecosystem of related sites, services and software that has vastly amplified its power and flexibility. There is a bit of a learning curve here because picking and mastering the right tools for your business takes time, but you'll get the hang of it.

I did, during months of research for this book, and I can assure you a Ph.D. is not needed.

A Few Twitter Basics

Here's how to get started with Twitter:

Create an account at twitter.com. This only takes a few minutes, but you'll want to give careful thought to the username. Depending on how you'll use Twitter, it can be your company's name, the name of your product or service, or the name of the person who will be using it the most. Regardless, you'll want to make clear that this account is associated with your firm so that it won't be confused with a personal Twitter account.

Upload a picture. Twitter's generic icon won't cut it. Find a roughly square-shaped picture that is colorful and catchy, yet clearly conveys your company identity. Keep it simple, since the image will be displayed in a small size and fine details will be lost.

Fill in your info. You want to clearly convey who you are, so spend a bit of time with your "one-line bio" and pick the best possible web address (it's good to keep it short). You will also find text fields for an email address, your location and other particulars.

Start tweeting! The only way to get the hang of Twitter is to plunge in. You are limited to 140 characters per tweet, so there's no cause for writer's block. Just tweet something! This can be seen by anyone on Twitter, and particularly by anyone who "follows" you.

Attract a following. You will soon attract Twitter followers (those who add you to their lists of favorite Twitter accounts), so make certain you don't miss new arrivals. You can configure Twitter to send you an automated email when someone starts following you.

You can follow, too. If someone follows you, you can follow right back. You'll have the ability to exchange private (or "direct") messages with those followers. Set up Twitter to email you whenever a DM comes in, and click the "direct messages" tab to see these.

Engage in conversations. Direct messages are fine, but the best exchanges take place in public view. Want to address people directly in a tweet, or respond to something they've tweeted? Type the persons' usernames preceded by "@" symbol at the beginning of your tweets, and they will soon see them in the "Replies" sections of their Twitter pages. They can respond by typing your username preceded by "@" at the beginning of their tweets.

Need more basics? Here are several excellent Twitter primers or launching pads:

Twitter in Plain English.[55] This terrific video by Common Craft is required viewing for all new Twitter users. You can watch a small web-based version for free, or purchase a higher-quality version for sharing within your organization.

Tweeternet.[56] This site is essential browsing for Twitter novices as well as experienced users, who will find Twitter introductions, how-to guides and much more.

Zappos on Twitter.[57] Zappos, profiled in Chapter Two, is so bullish about Twitter that it wants everyone to learn about it. To that end, it has created a "Beginner's Quick Start Guide and Tutorial to Using Twitter."

Search Engine Guide.[58] This blog has a detailed series of posts by Jennifer Laycock on how to get started with Twitter, and tap its power.

The Big Juicy Twitter Guide.[59] How can you resist a site with that name? This multi-part primer by Caroline Middlebrook is pretty good, too.

Twitter 101.[60] Online-community strategist Connie Bensen provides a roundup of Twitter-related resources.

Twitter Search (Formerly Summize)

Now that you're up to speed, let's dig into another essential Twitter feature: search. Your company will want to know what is being said about it on Twitter. You may also want to find folks to follow by scouring the Twitterverse using specific search criteria.

---

55 commoncraft.com/Twitter
56 tweeternet.com
57 twitter.zappos.com/start
58 searchengineguide.com/jennifer-laycock
/part-one-from-twits-to-tweeple-why-i-emb.php
59 caroline-middlebrook.com/blog/twitter-guide
60 conscientiousness/blog/2008/09/26/twitter-101

Searching Twitter chatter for specific words and phrases used to be quite a hassle—blame a Spartan Twitter design for this—but powerful search tools later appeared to turbocharge this essential task.

The best of these was called Summize until earlier this year when Twitter bought out the fabulous Twitter-focused search engine and set about incorporating its functionality into the main Twitter site. (As of this writing, the two remained mostly separate.)

I became a Summize addict because of its elegant interface and uncanny (if not flawless) ability to find what I wanted. It is essentially the Google of the Twitterverse, and served me well during the writing of this book because of my need to search for relevant tweets.

What's being said about your company or your product? Punch in the term; it's that easy.

Other things I like about Summize—now called Twitter Search[61]—include:

People searching. What did a particular Twitter user tweet? What did others say about that Twitter user, or to that user? It's easy to find out.

To pull up any user's tweets, just plug in his or her username. In my case, that would be "jojeda" (without those quotes). If you're curious what I have been tweeting lately, type "jojeda" into the search window. Bam! My tweets appear in reverse chronological order, newest tweets first.

Add the "@" symbol to the beginning of my username to see what has been said to me, or about me. If someone is addressing me directly in a tweet, he or she will start it with "@jojeda" to tip me off. Similarly, if someone makes a reference to me in a tweet, he or she will customarily place "@jojeda" somewhere within the body of that posting. Search for "@jojeda" and you will find all Twitter tweets directed at me, and about me. Easy!

---

61 search.twitter.com

Message threading. If a tweet you pull up as part of a keyword search is part of a multi-tweet conversation, Twitter Search will show it in its results. Click "show conversation" at the end of a tweet, and the full exchange (or, at least, most of it) will appear as a drop-down menu. This is handy, though irrelevant tweets are often inserted into conversations.

Trending topics. What's hot in the Twitterverse? Twitter Search displays a list of words and phrases corresponding to popular topics of the moment. The "Dark Knight" film and Apple's iPhone were favorites at the time I was writing this book. It was via the trending topics that I learned of the liberation of Ingrid Betancourt, a Colombian politician being held captive by Leftist guerrillas, in early July. A southern-California earthquake in late July was another hot trending topic. So, briefly, was an August discussion about this still-unfinished book (the transcript of that Twitter-based chat now comprises Chapter Five).

Advanced search. Twitter Search conceals lots of power under the hood. An advanced-search area lets you fine-tune searches by multiple criteria, such as word combinations, hashtags (which are words preceded by the "#" symbol), dates and places (based on the geographical information users supply for themselves in their Twitter accounts).

More Twitter Searching

Twitter Search is far from the only way to scour the Twittersphere. Here are a few other options:

Tweet Scan.[62] Often cited alongside Twitter Search as a terrific general-purpose Twitter search engine, Tweet Scan adds several automated-delivery options. Users can set up email alerts, for instance, so that search results are periodically delivered to their inboxes. Tweet Scan also offers an option to download all your old tweets for safekeeping.

---

62 tweetscan.com

Quotably.[63] In an approach similar to the "show conversation" feature on Twitter Search, Quotably shows a Twitter user's exchanges with others. I found Quotably to be wildly inaccurate in compiling conversation threads, but it does have a "fix threading" feature.

Twemes.[64] Aforementioned hashtags (words preceded by the "#" symbol) are often used by groups of Twitter users to conduct conversations around a shared subject; inserting an agreed-upon hashtag into relevant tweets lets all members of the group follow the topical thread. It's easy to find hashtags in Twitter Search, but Twemes is a bit better suited for this because of a "start live update" feature that eliminates manual page refreshing.

Twellow.[65] This is a sort of Yellow Pages of the Twitterverse because it groups users by categories. To be categorized, enter your Twitter username and then select all relevant listings. As a newspaper writer, I am under "news," "media" and "news/newspapers."

TwitDir.[66] This combo search engine and user directory had indexed more than 3 million Twitter users as of this writing (it only lists those who have public accounts, not those who keep tweets private). TwitDir is then able to spit out listings, such as the 100 most-followed users, those who follow the most folks, those who update the most, and more.

TwitScoop.[67] Emulating the "trending topics" in Twitter Search, TwitScoop scours the Twitterverse and analyzes which words and phrases are hot; it displays these in a word "cloud," with more-popular terms shown larger. (It's mesmerizing to watch words grow and shrink in real time.) TwitScoop has other bells and whistles. Search for a username, and it will display a graph of that person's tweeting frequency over time. Search for an activity hashtag to automatically see updates as they're posted.

---

63 quotably.com
64 twemes.com
65 twellow.com
66 twitdir.com
67 twitscoop.com

TweetVolume.[68] Enter words or phrases to see how often they're mentioned on Twitter. This is handy for companies that want to see how often they come up in the Twitterverse. You can enter up to five terms or sets of terms in separate boxes, and then have results for the five combined in a bar graph. I recently conducted a sample search for the five companies in Chapter Four; Zappos was champ with 18,800 mentions, followed by Dell (11,200), JetBlue (7,200) Comcast (7,100) and Whole Foods (5,460). The rankings do fluctuate wildly.

A Twitter-Search Specialist

While many companies and public-relations agencies do all their own keyword searches on Twitter and other internet services, some bring in search specialists for this. Canadian tech firm Radian6 is regarded as one of the finest online-analysis companies, with a star-studded customer list that includes such PR agencies as Weber Shandwick, Golin Harris, Brodeur Partners and Carmichael Lynch, as well as companies of all sizes (such as Dell).

Why hire Radian6? "The Summizes and Tweet Scans don't necessarily get all the tweets," David Alston, the firm's Vice President of Marketing, told me. "Our clients want to know everything, capture everything."

Radian6 captures everything, he says, because it has a direct arrangement with Twitter to access its ever-updating database of user tweets in real time—it's like a Twitter firehose plugged into Radian6's New Brunswick headquarters.

Its customers then get access to the tweet stream and can run any number of specialized searches—for their company names or brands, for instance—using web tools Radian6 provides. The web tools scour the rest of the internet, too, and assist users in analyzing the results. This is priceless data, Alston said, because it gives his customers an accurate sense of what is being said online—on blogs, in forums, on picture- and video-sharing sites as well as on Twitter and other social networks—about their brands and products.

---

68 tweetvolume.com

This allows a company to react quickly when "someone says its 'Brand X really upset me,'" Alston said.

Radian6 is an increasingly crowded field of social-media-monitoring services that include the likes of New York-based Techrigy.

So Whom Should I Follow?

The obvious way for a company to begin developing a Twitter following is to look for mentions of its name or the names of its products or services. Twitter Search and other search engines are great for this. Once the company finds Twitter users who are talking up its brand, for better or for worse, it can follow those users.

There are other ways to identify potential prospects, however. The following tools are especially useful:

TwitterLocal.[69] Many companies will want to locate and follow Twitter users in specific areas (their own, for instance). TwitterLocal makes this simple. Punch in a ZIP code or a city name. Specify a radius (of 1 mile or greater). The site spits up a list of relevant users. This site also has a Leader Board page, ranking the world's cities by tweeting frequency.

TwitterPacks.[70] This wiki-style website ("wiki" means anyone can modify it) cleverly groups users by categories. These include locations, companies, big national events and "identities" (such as races, religions and ages). While such packs aren't comprehensive (neither the company nor geographical listings are anywhere near complete, for instance), they're a great way to find Twitter users who matter the most to you.

Twitter Brand Index.[71] This is a definitive directory of brands in the corporate, media and academic spheres, among others. A superb way for a company to develop a Twitter strategy is to follow its peers and

---

69 twitterlocal.net
70 twitterpacks.pbwiki.com
71 socialbrandindex.com

learn from their example. You'll find your peers here. Get your Twitter accounts listed here, as well. Laura Fitton of Pistachio Consulting links to this and other brands-on-Twitter listings on her popular blog.[72]

Twitterati.[73] Who's who in the Twitterverse? The Alltop network of themed pages, each with recent links to top sites in a particular category, includes a Twitterati page. Many of the major Twitter users are featured there. These include social-media guru Chris Brogan and Leo Laporte, the famed host of many popular tech shows on the radio and internet.

Twitterholic.[74] This directory also identifies the Twitterverse's top denizens, but purely based on how many followers they've amassed. Topping the listing as of mid-October was presidential candidate Barack Obama (rival John McCain was nowhere to be found) and famed tech entrepreneur Kevin Rose, followed by Leo Laporte. The NASA Mars Phoenix lander, a favorite of Twitter cofounder Biz Stone, was ranked seventh.

Twitter Apps For Tweeting

For some Twitter users, the standard web interface is more than enough. Others prefer to install Twitter-related software on their computers and mobile devices. Such applications provide added features and flexibility for business users. Here are several of your options:

Twhirl.[75] Running on Windows PCs or Macintosh machines, the software shows tweets and other information in a fun, colorful vertical window that users typically place on the left or right sides of their computer screens. Twhirl incorporates handy features such as searching (via either Twitter Search or Tweet Scan) and shortening of too-lengthy web addresses within tweets. It is priceless for those with multiple Twitter accounts because it lets them keep some or all of those accounts open simultaneously, each in its own window.

---

72 pistachioconsulting.com/brands-on-twitter
73 twitter.alltop.com
74 twitterholic.com
75 twhirl.org

TweetDeck.[76] Like Twhirl, this app runs on either PC or Mac (a feat made possible with a bit of "cross-platform" software called Adobe AIR, which installs itself automatically). TweetDeck differs dramatically from Twhirl in how it displays and organizes its Twitter information. Using a multi-column arrangement, it gives users the flexibility to organize followers into groups. Twitter replies and search results show up in their own columns. Some have found TweetDeck's design to be unwieldy, but it was popular at press time.

Twitterific.[77] A favorite of Macintosh users, this application is even more playful than Twhirl. It incorporates Mac-specific features such as an unread-tweet count in the Mac OS X application dock, Growl notifications (which are little windows that pop up when new tweets come in) and a range of keyboard shortcuts. A mobile version of Twitterific for use on Apple's iPhone was offered last summer, and became a hit. Both versions of Twitterific are made available in paid and free-with-ads versions.

More iPhone apps. Twitter apps are hugely popular on Apple's handset, which is really a minicomputer running a version of the Mac OS X operating system. The Twitter apps fall into two categories: web-based "apps," which are really specialized websites, and apps consisting of actual software installed on the phone.

The aforementioned Twitterific falls into the software-app category. So do Twinkle and Twittelator and Twitterfon, which all function as mobile Twitter interfaces. Specialized Twitter apps for the iPhone perform useful functions such as searching (Summizer) and mapping (Twittervision). To get any of these, download and install Apple's iTunes, then look for the apps in the App Store section of the iTunes Store.

In the web-app category, you'll want Hahlo.[78] This mobile-web version of Twitter was my favorite way to access the service on an iPhone as of this writing. Twitter has its own mobile-web interface,[79] which is much simpler than Hahlo but has the virtue of working on virtually any mobile handset with web-browsing capabilities.

---

76 tweetdeck.com
77 iconfactory.com/software/twitterrific
78 hahlo.com
79 m.twitter.com

Twitter on other phones. Other kinds of cell phones have their own Twitter options. Tiny Twitter[80] is one popular choice for BlackBerrys and Windows Mobile phones as well as any phone capable of running Java-based applications. Some BlackBerry users prefer TwitterBerry.[81] Cell-phone users don't need Twitter apps, though, because their tweets can be transmitted via text messaging (or SMS); wireless charges may apply. Twitter does not work via instant messaging, however. It did at one time, but Twitter dropped this feature and recently warned that restoring it wouldn't be a top priority.

More Software and Services

Firefox add-ons.[82] The Firefox browser is popular partly because of its plug-in system that lets third parties add capabilities. Thousands of such software "extensions" exist; a number of them are Twitter-related. These include Twitbin and TwitterFox, which add a Twitter interface to the browser for sending and receiving tweets, and TwitterBar, which lets users post to Twitter in the browser's address field.

Flock.[83] A browser based on Firefox, Flock needs no Twitter-related extensions because it has a built-in ability to monitor a Twitter account. It's called "the social web browser" for this reason (it can scan other services, like Facebook, YouTube, MySpace and Flickr, as well).

TwitterCounter.[84] For many Twitteraholics, follower-count watching is an obsession. This site is useful for tracking your follower count over time, and catching sudden dips that might be the result of Twitter malfunctions (a not-uncommon occurrence) and not people "unfollowing" you.

---

80 tinytwitter.com
81 orangatame.com/products/twitterberry
82 addons.mozilla.org/en-US/firefox
83 flock.com
84 twittercounter.com

Digsby.[85] For those wanting to monitor email and instant messaging as well as Twitter and other social-networking services (such as Facebook and MySpace), Digsby provides a unified and elegant interface. It was Windows-only as of this writing, but the publisher said a Macintosh version was in the works.

Twitterator.[86] Following other Twitter users one by one is a time-consuming hassle, so Twitterator was born to make this faster. Enter a bunch of usernames and click to follow them all; fast and easy.

My Tweeple.[87] Keeping track of your followers and those who follow you is a hassle in Twitter's too-basic interface, so try My Tweeple. You can easily see whether someone you are following also happens to be following you, for instance. Click to follow, block or unfollow someone; these changes are promptly reflected on Twitter.

Tweet Pro.[88] This is Windows-based Twitter-searching software intended for those who need to keep track of certain words or topics in the Twitterverse. Search engines do this, too, but Tweet Pro adds additional features such as grid-style search-result organizing, support for multiple accounts, automated following of user who meet particular criteria, and more. Oddly, you don't buy the software, but pony up $9.95 a day or $19.95 for 30 days.

NetVibes.[89] This is not a Twitter-related service but more of a customizable home page that displays a variety of widgets containing news headlines, videos, pictures and more. This site comes in handy for Twitter users who have two or more accounts they need to follow simultaneously. On their NetVibes page, they can display a continually updating widget for each of those accounts, side by side.

M.A.T.T.[90] Short for Multiple Account Twitter Tweeting, the site lets you post to several Twitter accounts at once. Designate a primary account and one or more secondary ones. Then tweet once to some or all of

---

85 digsby.com
86 twitterator.org
87 mytweeple.com
88 soxialize.com
89 netvibes.com
90 themattinator.com

them—no more logging out of one account and logging into another. This is great for businesses that have to juggle multiple accounts. M.A.T.T. is a favorite of mine because it is useful, elegantly executed and gorgeously designed (though occasionally prone to technical hiccups).

Monitter.[91] Wondering what is being said about a particular topic—right this second—on Twitter? This clever service lets you plug in three keywords, then see relevant tweets appear in real time. You can even make this geographically specific by entering a place identifier (such as a city or identifier) and a radius in miles or kilometers.

TweetLater.[92] This Twitter-scheduling service lets you compose a tweet now and post it at a future day and time of your choosing. This is a boon if you want to release a steady stream of tweets but you're going to be on a plane or otherwise incommunicado. Line up a series of pre-composed tweets, and decide when they go live. TweetLater does the rest.

TweetBeep.[93] Get email alerts when you, your company, your product or website get mentioned on Twitter.

TwitterMail.[94] Wouldn't it be great to post a tweet simply by sending an email? With TwitterMail, you can do just that.

TweetStats.[95] Enter your Twitter username and this service plots out your Twitter activity as a series of bar graphs, as well as in the form of a word-based "tweet cloud" with more-frequent terminology shown larger.

GroupTweet.[96] Turn Twitter into a private messaging platform for work groups. Once members of a group are registered with the service, any member can post to the group's communal account, and only members of that group will see the tweets. This allows for effortless collaboration on group projects when members are not all in the same place.

---

91 monitter.com
92 tweetlater.com
93 tweetbeep.com
94 twittermail.com
95 tweetstats.com

Twitter via RSS Subscriptions

RSS feeds are another fantastic way to stay on top of Twitter. RSS is short for "Really Simple Syndication," and it really is simple once you get the hang of it.

With RSS, you subscribe to a site's "feed"—Practically every site out there, from huge ones like the New York Times to humble blogs, now has a feed. You assemble all your feed subscriptions in a centralized location, known as an RSS reader. Some readers, like Google Reader,[97] are web-based. Others consist of software you install on a computer; options include FeedDemon[98] for Windows and NetNews-Wire[99] for Macintosh. Your RSS reader will keep you abreast of updates to all of your favorite sites, via their feeds.

So what does this have to do with Twitter? Users of the service have subscription options galore. On the main Twitter site, each user's page has an RSS feed. By subscribing to the feeds of all Twitter users you regard as important, you can stay abreast of updates to their tweet streams in your RSS reader.

You can also subscribe to RSS searches. Conduct a search using keywords, and then take a careful look at the page with the search results. If you used Twitter Search, you will see a "feed for this query" link on the upper right; click that to subscribe. Other Twitter-type search engines, such as Tweet Scan and TwitterLocal, include RSS options.

You can even use RSS to keep your Twitter followers abreast of changes to your blog, if you have one. Use TwitterFeed[100] for this. Once you have this service set up, a new post to your blog will generate an automated tweet that will let your followers know about the new blog content.

---

96 grouptweet.com
97 reader.google.com
98 newsgator.com/individuals/feeddemon
99 newsgator.com/individuals/netnewswire
100 twitterfeed.com

Twitter junkies who are also RSS junkies may want to check out Cullect,[101] a web-based RSS reader that, developer Garrick Van Buren says, "is smart about Twitter and Twitter streams." If a tweet links to a video or a photo, for instance, that content is embedded automatically within the reader. Cullect has a built-in URL shortener, and it autoexpands shortened URLs within tweets. It lets users log in to the site using their Twitter identities. It even lets them reply to tweets from within the site, and can tweet to multiple accounts.

A List of Resource Lists

Twitter is now so popular that the sheer number of related sites, services and software is far too big to list here. So below is a brief list of lists—pointers to the top Twitter-related resource sites. Consult them regularly for all the latest Twitter downloads, tips and trends.

Pistachio Consulting.[102] Laura Fitton's site is important for companies that grapple with Twitter and other microblogging services. Along with her consulting services focused on "microsharing," Fitton provides a wealth of no-cost information via her relentless linking and personal research. Key posts on her blog include a "Getting Started with Twitter"[103] linkfest and a Twitter-for-business reading list.[104] These and other vital posts are found on Fitton's featured-article page.[105]

Twitter Fan Wiki.[106] This is a gigantic directory of all things Twitter. Its lists range from the practical to the whimsical: apps, Twitter-related groups and clubs, Twitter users that aren't human, mentions of Twitter in the media, and more. There's also a guide to Twitter etiquette (listed under "important stuff").

Twitterholics.[107] This often-updated blog "for all those obsessed with Twitter" offers a steady stream of pointers to the latest Twitter tips, tools and news.

---

101 cullect.com
102 pistachioconsulting.com
103 pistachioconsulting.com/getting-started-on-twitter
104 pistachioconsulting.com/twitter-for-business-reading-list
105 pistachioconsulting.com/microsharing/featured-articles
106 twitter.pbwiki.com

Twittermaven.[108] This blog promises "everything you ever wanted to know about Twitter."

Twitter Blog.[109] This is Twitter's official blog, and a good way to keep track of Twitter developments, trends, services and applications.

Alternatives to Twitter

Twitter's popularity (and to, some extent, its unreliability) has spawned competitors that claim to offer better capabilities along with greater stability and ease of use. None could boast a user base as large as Twitter's as of this writing, though, nor a vast ecosystem of software and services like that built around Twitter. Still, it's always nice to have choice.

Should companies pay attention to any of these Twitter rivals? Some have more business relevance than others.

FriendFeed.[110] Though often cited as a Twitter alternative, FriendFeed is a different sort of social-networking service.

For one thing, it's an alternate way to view Twitter content, as well as content from other sites. FriendFeed is an "aggregator" where users can collect the information they post on their blogs, bookmarking sites and photo or video sites, along with their social networks, including Twitter. FriendFeed supported about three dozen specific sites and services as of this writing. It's not unlike an RSS reader in this regard; in fact, FriendFeed users can pull in any RSS feed and add that content to their FriendFeed pages.

So how is FriendFeed "social," à la Twitter? Users can subscribe to each other (much as they follow each other on Twitter). This is a great way for one user to keep abreast with what another user has posted on all of his or her services and sites. Following too many people on FriendFeed can lead to information overload, though.

---

107 twitterholics.com
108 twittermaven.blogspot.com
109 blog.twitter.com
110 friendfeed.com

FriendFeed has the added benefit of built-in text discussions so users can have extensive conversations about what's occurring in their lives and on their various sites and services. FriendFeed even has a "rooms" feature for self-contained discussions among those who share a common interest (members of a wedding party, for instance, or fans of the Green Bay Packers). Rooms can be public or private.

Companies are getting on FriendFeed, much as they've embraced Twitter (though, as of this writing, to a lesser extent). These include Comcast[111] and the Ford Motor Company.[112]

FriendFeed fans include Steve Rubel, Senior Vice President and Director of Insights at Edelman Digital, part of the Edelman public-relations giant. He thinks FriendFeed is a solution to social-network fragmentation. Such services are so simple to create that many of them have sprung up, isolating users in various "wells," he said. FriendFeed brings such services and their users together. As a result, it could achieve Google-like popularity eventually, Rubel believes. He recently noted:

steverubel: I now have over 5000 following me on FriendFeed—60% of what I have on Twitter.

I'll confess to being ambivalent about FriendFeed, though, because of its awkward (though recently updated) look and the vast amount of information it tends to throw at its users. As I put it in a tweet:

jojeda: How do folks follow even a handful of web-savvy pals on FriendFeed without their brains exploding from information overload? I don't get it.

Wondering who's who on FriendFeed? The Alltop network of themed sites, mentioned earlier in this chapter in connection with its Twitterati super-user site, has a similar site showcasing the top FriendFeed users—It's called Frienderati.[113]

---

111 friendfeed.com/comcastcares
112 friendfeed.com/fordmotorcompany
113 frienderati.alltop.com

Utterli.[114] Twitter is text. That's it. So Twitter-like services have emerged to exploit other flavors of expression, such as audio and video. Utterli, in particular, has become popular among social-media types because it gives them the option to post audio clips as well as photos, video clips and text (all referred to as "utters" in Utterli parlance).

These are posted to the Utterli site, or to blogs and social-networking sites (like Twitter, in the form of links within tweets) and to photo- and video-sharing sites (like Flickr and YouTube). In short, it's a way to blast all manner of content, still or animated, to all the places where you customarily share information with others. This is typically done from cell phones, which is why the service refers to itself as "mobile multimedia discussions," but it can also be done from a computer with a microphone or webcam.

Utterli (originally called Utterz) has grown popular enough to merit an Utterati[115] page on the Alltop site network.

Public-relations professionals who champion Twitter are also favoring Utterli. One such P.R. pro is Albert Maruggi (author of this book's afterword, and also featured in Chapter Five) of Minnesota's Provident Partners public-relations and social-media agency. He became a prolific Utterli user earlier this year. He said he found it useful for posting off-the-cuff ideas and covering live events. Just as Twitter has become a fast alternative to full-scale blogging, he added, Utterli has become a supplement to full-scale podcasts (which are radio- or TV-like programs distributed on the internet).

Utterli can be useful at companies, Maruggi believes, for work teams who set up private "audio channels" much as Twitter is sometimes used for work-group communication and collaboration. He has been encouraging his clients to use Utterli.

Kel Kelly of the Boston-area Kel & Partners agency also recently warmed to Utterli as a complement to her prolific tweeting. She refers to Utterli as "Twitter on steroids" because it lets her blast out several

---

114 Utterli.com
115 utterati.alltop.com

utters—text, photos or video—on a single topic and assemble them as a "mashup" in one place. Now she's trying to get her clients interested in Utterli.

Pownce.[116] One of several so-called Twitter clones, Pownce had added features that have made it moderately popular. It has the built-in ability to share files and calendar events with others. Conversations around a shared topic are easier to conduct than on Twitter, too, courtesy of Pownce's built-in discussion features (not unlike those on FriendFeed). These are potentially useful among members of a work group if these are not all in the same place. There's Pownce desktop software as well as a mobile-browser incarnation.

Jaiku.[117] This Google-owned service is very much like Twitter, with a key difference: It pales in popularity. It lacks a vast ecosystem of software and services like the one built around Twitter. It does have useful features such as "channels" (an automated version of Twitter's hashtag system for keeping track of joint discussions) and the ability to pull in the contents of RSS feeds.

Identi.ca.[118] Bearing maybe the greatest superficial resemblance to Twitter of all Twitter clones, Identi.ca boasts a crucial difference under the hood: It's built atop "open source" computer code that anyone can use. This means individuals or companies could set up Identi.ca-like services on their own networked hardware if they did not want to rely on the centralized version, yet retain access to their Indenti.ca friends. As Identi.ca explains on its site:

"The goal here is autonomy—you deserve the right to manage your own on-line presence. If you don't like how Identi.ca works, you can take your data and the source code and set up your own server (or move your account to another one)."

---

116 pownce.com
117 jaiku.com
118 identi.ca

Identi.ca remained a work in progress as of this writing, but showed potential as a way to decentralize Twitter-style microblogging (keeping in mind that Twitter's technical issues are largely a result of its overtaxed centralized servers) and let users post to other services (like Twitter). This is a service to watch.

Identi.ca uses Laconica software that others are free to use and adapt it to their needs. A variety of Laconica-based microblogging services have recently emerged. These include the TWiT Army, founded by tech broadcaster and podcaster Leo Laporte.[119]

If you use Identi.ca or other leading Laconica-based services, rely on the previously mentioned Tweet Scan for keyword searching. This search engine was set up to scour 10 Laconica services (including Identi.ca) along with Twitter as of this writing.

Plurk.[120] This one takes Twitter's vertical-text approach and lays it on its side—literally. Users scan their timelines, made up of icon-style posts called "plurks," from left to right instead of top to bottom a la Twitter. Some like this approach but others find it awkward.

Plurks, like tweets, are limited to 140 characters. Plurk adds a few bells and whistles, like discussions within plurks, color-coded "qualifiers" that show emotion or intent (<feels> or <thinks>), automatic thumbnailing of picture or video links, and the ability to create groups called "cliques" composed of folks who share an interest.

"Twitter For the Enterprise"

As this book went to press, buzz was building around Twitter-like services tailored to the workplace and not the masses. Upstart firms like Yammer[121] and Present.ly[122] proposed to revitalize communication among colleagues within companies by giving them Twitter-like tools tailored to their organizations, along with greater privacy and security than the too-public Twitter can provide.

---

119 army.twit.tv
120 plurk.com
121 yammer.com
122 presentlyapp.com

I dabbled a bit with both Yammer and Present.ly, setting up test networks at my Pioneer Press workplace using a couple of internal email identities I control.

I liked how getting started with Yammer was simply a matter of entering one of my work emails to get my work-related network (using my employer's pioneerpress.com domain name) off the ground. Anyone else could join in by entering his or her Pioneer Press email address and becoming registered with the service.

Present.ly gave me a bit more control over the process as the default administrator of the internal microblogging network. I had the power to approve new members and so forth, and I liked how users weren't required to be using the pioneerpress.com domain name (meaning designated outsiders could potentially join in).

Yammer garnered a great deal of publicity over the summer and fall as winner of the prestigious TechCrunch 50 award.[123] Present.ly, though, made a better impression on such tech commentators as ZDNet's Jennifer Leggio (author of this book's foreword).[124]

Yammer and Present.ly at press time were a part of a large and rapidly growing category of microblogging services for the workplace. Keep up with this via such sites as Jeremiah Owyang's Web Strategy[125] and Laura Fitton's Pistachio Consulting.[126]

Posting to Multiple Services

Some companies, wanting to be thorough, might want to post not just on Twitter but on similar services (like the ones described above). This can be a hassle, though, because it requires submitting the same information repeatedly, in the form of a tweet, plurk, utter and so on.

---

123 techcrunch.com/2008/09/10/yammer-takes-techcrunch50s-top-prize
124 blogs.zdnet.com/feeds/?p=237
125 web-strategist.com/blog/2008/09/08
/list-of-enterprise-microblogging-tools-twitter-for-the-intranet
126 pistachioconsulting.com/list-of-internal-microsharing-tools

Thank goodness for services that largely automate this thankless duty. You compose and submit once, and publish to multiple places, automatically. Here are different ways to do this:

Ping.fm.[127] This service bills itself as "a simple service that makes updating your social networks a snap." It supported nearly two dozen services as of this writing—including Twitter, Pownce, Jaiku, Plurk, FriendFeed and Identi.ca—and even Yammer. It allowed updating via email, instant messaging, text messaging and Apple's iPhone, among others.

HelloTxt.[128] Emulating Ping.fm, though with a slightly different mix of services, this one also supports obvious ones like Twitter, Jaiku, Pownce, Plurk, FriendFeed and Identi.ca. It does Yammer, too. The service works via email, text messaging and mobile browsers.

Posty.[129] This is a piece of software for Windows or Macintosh that serves the same role as the web-based Ping.fm and Hello.Txt. Using an elegant little window, you can post to Twitter as well as to Jaiku, Pownce, FriendFeed and Indenti.ca.

Blog It.[130] If your company has a presence on the popular Facebook social network, or is otherwise familiar with it, this one is for you. The Blog It widget (or "application" in the Facebook context) from blog-service company Six Apart, will post to Twitter, Jaiku, Pownce and Friend-Feed, as well as to blogs. A web-based version of Blog It works on Apple's iPhone.

Socialthing.[131] Combining elements of FriendFeed and the multi-service publishing tools cited earlier in this section, Socialthing is a way to keep abreast of activity on a Twitter account as well as in Pownce, Plurk and other services. It also lets users post to Twitter, Pownce, Plurk and others. Socialthing was recently acquired by online giant AOL.

---

127 ping.fm
128 hellotxt.com
129 spreadingfunkyness.com/posty
130 typepad.com/blogit
131 socialthing.com

Twhirl.[132] The aforementioned Twitter desktop software for Windows and Macintosh not only posts to multiple Twitter accounts, but to Identi.ca, Pownce, Jaiku and FriendFeed, as well.

Flock.[133] The aforementioned "social browser" based on Firefox merits a repeat mention because it keeps users on top of Pownce as well as Twitter.

---

132 twhirl.org
133 flock.com

I Live My Own Book

Writing this book got me so excited about Twitter and its business uses that, last summer, I fired off an email to my boss. "I'd like to speak with you about a social-media strategy for the paper," I told St. Paul Pioneer Press editor Thom Fladung. "We aren't on Twitter, for starters."

We needed to be, I told to him in a follow-up meeting, to better connect with our existing readers and lure new ones. The service is about relationships, I said. Twitter could help us nurture reader ties.

A week or so later, Thom called me into his office. That Twitter thing, he said, good idea. Why don't you do it?

The editor (think Lou Grant with a full head of hair) had a particular use in mind. St. Paul would soon host the Republican National Convention, and it was all hands on deck at the paper for this once-in-a-lifetime event. Adding a Twitter piece to our exhaustive coverage would make sense and be simple to implement, Thom said.

I agreed, and promptly created a @PiPress account with an avatar of the paper's signature bulldog holding a newspaper in its mouth.

After months spent focusing on businesses that use Twitter, I had suddenly become such a company. (Note that while my longtime @jojeda persona is informally associated with my employer, @PiPress would become its official mouthpiece.)

My mind was racing at this point. I had learned much about how a firm should or should not use Twitter. How would I apply this wisdom? Companies can use Twitter effectively in a mind-boggling variety of ways, but what approach would be appropriate in my case?

I was in for a wild ride. How I used Twitter would evolve over an exhausting week, with John McCain and Sarah Palin holding court inside the Xcel Energy convention center as protesters clashed with police on downtown streets. I was also in for a bit of press-world acclaim as my Twitter use got noticed around the nation, and within my own workplace.

Promote, promote, promote. As the newspaper's RNC coverage geared up in the week before the convention, I began promoting it on Twitter. This was an obvious first step and a vital one: Many Twitter users depend on their tweet feeds to keep up on the latest news. I gave @PiPress followers links to everything in the newspaper about the RNC—before, during and after the convention.

PiPress: Pigeons shooed away. Cabs scrubbed. Red, white and blue bunting hung. Dang it, we're ready.
http://twincities.com/ci_10343164 #RNC08

Don't forget the hashtag. I knew my @PiPress following would be minute at first. But through the magic of hashtagging, I could boost my Twitterverse readership immediately and exponentially.

By putting "#RNC08" (minus the quotes) in all of my RNC-related tweets, I guaranteed myself a wide audience since that was the agreed-upon hashtag for those wanting to keep track of RNC-related chatter in the Twitterverse. My RNC tweets would come up in any keyword search for #RNC08. Better yet, press organizations like the Poynter Institute and C-SPAN set up websites or Twitter feeds to repackage or redistribute #RNCO8 content.

(To watch history unfold, plug "PiPress" and "#RNC08" into any Twitter search engine.)

Be a human, not a drone. As a mouthpiece of a corporation (my newspaper is owned by the big MediaNews Group chain of papers), I was fearful of coming across as impersonal. So I injected some of personality into the @PiPress feed. I made clear who was tweeting and how readers could contact me. Here is how the account's bio blurb read at the time:

"Follow the St. Paul Pioneer Press during the Republican National Convention in downtown St. Paul. Tweets by @jojeda.
Contact: social@pioneerpress.com"

I also deviated regularly from my newspaper-promotion work to inject a little personality and give readers peeks inside the Pioneer Press:

PiPress: Pioneer Press intern arrives, immediately asks about Wi-Fi for use with his black MacBook. I like the guy already. But clean MB a bit, d00d.

PiPress: News flash: Pioneer Press editor Thom Fladung is on Twitter. He is @fladung. Not sure what he'll do (other than follow moi), give him ideas.

Follow, follow, follow. One tactical decision I had to make immediately: Would I engage in two-way conversations as a rule, or mostly push information outward? It is a common dilemma when firms set up Twitter accounts: Some use them for conversation, others for distribution. It soon became clear to me that @PiPress would primarily be a megaphone, not an intercom. Amid frantic RNC coverage, I simply would not have time for chitchat.

Nevertheless, I acknowledged @PiPress followers at every opportunity. If one followed me, I followed right back (usually within minutes). If someone addressed me directly, in the public twitter stream or privately via a direct message, I responded immediately and continued that conversation to a logical conclusion.

Improvise and adapt. This @PiPress tweeting took an unexpected turn before the RNC even began. I happened to be working the Saturday evening before the convention kicked off, so I immediately became aware of police raids on suspected RNC-protester hangouts.

Protest-rights groups also were using the #RNC08 hashtag, so I was able to follow along as the police moved from raid to raid. I was soon monitoring a number of crucial RNC-related Twitter accounts to better keep up as news unfolded, and feeding information to the Pioneer Press' public-safety writers as well as to @PiPress followers. I had become a kind of news dispatcher, in effect, with a beeping iPhone serving as a sort of police radio that flashed RNC-related tweets arriving as text messages. This was all just a bit surreal.

"Julio rocks!" one cop writer later wrote in all-staff email. "Julio kept track, via Twitter on up-to-the-second-raids and arrests, and kept us all plugged in... Big thanks to Julio."

Thom followed up in a staff memo: "I know that some of you have questioned the value of Twitter, what it means to us, how we can use it. This is how we should use it."

I was one of several local news outlets sending out raid-related news via Twitter. Media analyst David Brauer of MinnPost.com later wrote that "for raid coverage, Twitter was the place to be," partly because of @PiPress content.[134]

Stumble and regroup. My newsroom fame would be short-lived. As cop-and-protester activity continued during the RNC, I kept up my news-monitoring duties but stumbled badly at times. The Twitterverse was rife with rumors, and I sometimes sent cop writers on wild-goose chases based on bad information. I had become the boy who cried wolf.

"Is that from Twitter?" an editor suspiciously asked via email when I fed the newsroom a tip about mass arrests near the convention center. "Last time it was a false alarm," one of the police reporters chimed in. I had to convince them it was the real deal. I confirmed this by watching live web video from The Uptake,[135] a citizen journalism operation using camcorders and video-capable mobile phones—along with Twitter—for RNC coverage.

---

134 minnpost.com/davidbrauer/2008/08/31/3239
/for_raid_coverage_twitter_was_the_place_to_be
135 theuptake.org

Recover and soar. It dawned on several police reporters that they could follow RNC-related Twitter accounts themselves, right on their computers or cell phones, and make their own snap judgments about which Twitterverse tips to investigate. So they asked me for assistance in setting this up.

This was a breeze. Once I had their Twitter usernames and passwords, I could replicate my RNC source list within each of their accounts. They then had the option to monitor Twitter on their mobile web browsers, or activate their accounts' cell-phone features so they could get relevant tweets as text messages (as I did so effectively on my iPhone).

One top reporter didn't do any of this, but continued relying on me for tips. "Keep me Twittered," he told me in an email before heading out on his news-monitoring rounds.

Eyewitness news. Though much of my Twitter-related work was done at my Pioneer Press desk, I'd periodically dash outside to watch news being made. The Xcel Energy convention center was only a couple of blocks from the paper, after all, and protesting also occurred mostly nearby. This was enthralling, and also stressful as I watched my normally quiet neighborhood in turmoil. I said as much in often-opinionated tweeting:

PiPress: Scary to be average downtown pedestrian right now: Hordes of riot cops in heavy black gear, herds of gasmask-wearing cops on bicycles #RNC08

PiPress: As downtown resident, not a fun day for me. Heavily armed goon-like troops here! Rock-throwing anarchist types there! Sheesh. #RNC08

At one of several protests I watched unfold while tweeting on my iPhone, a Republican delegate gabbing on his phone apparently mistook me for a demonstrator and remarked how he wanted to "pound this Obama backer." Given that other journalists were gassed, roughed up and even arrested during the RNC, I guess I should feel fortunate.

The biggest protest by far occurred on the last night of the RNC, and I had my Twitter-monitoring system down pat by then. As police chased protesters in a department-store parking lot and dispatches came in from our reporters and photographers on the scene, I plugged them into Twitter to create a running narrative in a series of consecutive tweets:

PiPress: Police trying to disperse crowd. Protesters tried to get as far as University. Police didn't want that. So now it's a random horde..."

PiPress: ...all dispersed in Sears parking lot, and police are chasing down groups of them. They've arrested a couple already, just individuals..."

PiPress: ...not rounding up a group and arresting en masse."

Tweet like a madman. I hadn't forgotten about my newspaper-promotion efforts, which was the reason to start @PiPress in the first place. Anytime the paper ran any item about the RNC, online or in print, no matter how small, I'd describe it in a pithy tweet and link to it. I had no idea how exhausting this could be; I needed to stay up until well past 1 a.m. each night to snag that next day's stories as they hit my paper's site, then resume work at around sunrise after a few fitful hours of sleep. (Thanks, Thom, for all the overtime pay).

All that Twittering added up. On C-SPAN's #RNC08 page, accounts were ranked based on tweeting frequency. The @PiPress account soon took the lead, and never gave it up.[136] I'd ultimately tweet more than 700 times while on RNC duty while attracting nearly 300 followers (hardly spectacular by Twitterverse standards, but not to shabby for a few days of tweeting).

This got noticed. C-SPAN sent a congratulatory email at one point about my lead status: "Keep up the great tweeting, you are #1 on the Leader Board."

@PiPress was soon being written up by news outlets in Minnesota and around the nation. "The revolution will be Twittered," wrote the Minnesota Independent, a news site, citing the Pioneer Press and others.[137]

---

136 rnc08.c-span.org/?page_id=338
137 minnesotaindependent.com/7842/the-revolution-will-be-twittered

The media-focused Poynter Institute, in its RNC analysis, said Twitter was the "surprise star of RNC coverage." It observed that while the Minneapolis-based Star Tribune is the area's dominant paper, "the smaller Pioneer Press gets praise for navigating the Web 2.0 world."[138]

Twitter praise rolled in:

donmball: Is it just me or is PiPress mopping up the floor with the Strib on #rnc08 coverage? Makes this Eastsider proud.

malbiniak: hats off to @PiPress for covering the real stories going on around #rnc08 (and others)

mjkeliher: Attention please: Huge kudos to @MinnPostNow, @MNIndy, @TheUptake and @PiPress for *great* coverage around the convention. Well done, all.

My favorite bit of @PiPress praise came from a local blog called "Minneapolis Michael":

"...Every local media outlet needs to do what the Pioneer Press is doing. By using their Twitter account as a place to post links to stories and place them in context, it gives me a credible local source AND they are looked upon favorably by the Twitterverse."[139]

That's a good summation of what Thom and I aspired to do with @PiPress. We wanted to make the newspaper's RNC coverage more visible online, and generate excitement about it. I succeeded beyond my expectations.

OK, so now what? With RNC 2008 receding into history, I was left to ponder what to do with our Twitter account. Retiring it was unthinkable. As I was completing this epilogue, Thom and I were discussing exactly how @PiPress would stay active in the Twitterverse.

---

138 www.poynter.org/column.asp?id=31&aid=150242
139 minneapolismichael.tumblr.com/post/48397969
/how-twitter-changed-my-rnc-experience

Twitter and politics had become inseparable by that point. Twitter itself created an Election 2008 site at election.twitter.com to scour the Twitterverse for political chatter and display it in a format that updated automatically.

At my paper, meanwhile, a Twitter surge was under way as my once-skeptical coworkers began to embrace the service and adapt it to their needs.

Political writer Rachel Stassen-Berger is perhaps the best example of this. The veteran reporter and prolific blogger took to Twitter with gusto, spawning a @PolAnimal identity that is an offshoot of her Political Animal blog.

In a later, creative twist, she fashioned an @MNvotes identity to track local voter sentiment and polling-place activity on Nov. 4. This identity, which promoted the use of an #mnvotes hashtag, spawned a virtual firestorm of tweeting on and shortly after election day.

Twitter appears to have a promising future at the Pioneer Press, though some within the organization still regard it with a bit of caution and skepticism. I think they'll get over it.

Afterword by Albert Maruggi

Julio covers the uses of Twitter in a business environment succinctly and with a breadth that most businesses reading this book can adapt to their own objectives. Congratulations on a thoughtful compilation of work. I am grateful to be asked to write an afterword for a book on technology and social media because, in this space, there is always an afterward.

Twitter is Organic, Growing

Twitter, more than most social networks, is organic. It grows with each tweet, each new user, each new topic. For a business, it is important to understand that Twitter is not like any other medium they have used.

Each day, Twitter changes. If businesses have the right objectives, tactics and execution, Twitter will help that company change, as well. The organic nature of Twitter is about learning, sharing and relationships. Continual growth, driven by fresh ideas and people participating, means you should regularly search keywords to locate individuals talking about areas of interest to you. Learn about them by reading their profiles and follow the ones of most interest. One of the most important marketing lessons I have learned in 25 years of being in the profession came from a t-shirt. It said, "It's not who you know, it's who knows you." Twitter facilitates people knowing you.

Corporate Culture is Tested

You read here about businesses using Twitter to sell (a la @DellOutlet), but another real benefit comes when Twitter helps turn a mirror on a company. Such a reflection can spur individuals within the company to challenge corporate policies that do not make sense. This reflection can inspire them to enthusiastically embrace their corporate brand in a way that makes them come alive for the customer. Julio cites examples like Comcast, Dell and H&R Block that epitomize this trend.

Now the real test for Twitter—and social media in general—is whether traditional 20th-century corporations are able to incorporate the realities of social-media culture. This is one that includes many of their customers, their new employees, and most importantly, a shifting perspective of our society.

What is Business, After All?

Culturally, America is accepting the reality of blended obligations: work, kids, ailing parents, work weekends and an always accessible workforce. This is OK, as most have traded a structured 40-hour work week for freedom. Ironic as it seems, technology has allowed us to be both as connected and disconnected as necessary.

The culture of Twitter is a blender of human interactions—thoughts, opinions, questions, reactions. You send a tweet, maybe someone responds, maybe not. The President of Best Buy for Business, @dhemler, can share insights about business, dining experiences, and whether he likes Google Docs or the ZOHO equivalent.

Over time, when people and businesses fully engage and participate in social media, a quilt of humanity will be woven together. It's this spectrum of tweets that usually throw companies off and where traditional corporate types abandon the Twitter ship. What they fail to see is that society is moving toward the quilt, and away from the compartments.

The hurdle for businesses to overcome in order to fully benefit from social media is the giving—giving of their time, their ideas, their knowledge, favorite links that are helpful to others. Such an effort is likely to be returned tenfold. This is not the typical corporate mentality.

Today, many corporations think they need metrics to move. What has made Twitter so simple yet powerful is people can do it on their own... to explore the waters, to answer someone having a problem with his or her own business taking a too-official company line. You don't need approval to be helpful, America.

This is a change in society that social media is helping facilitate; you don't need approval to act, to think, to object, to advocate. This is an "I think, therefore I tweet" philosophy.

A Celebration of Humanity

Traditionally, American business is the last place you'd hear an admission of error. There are plenty of legitimate reasons for this; a too-litigious society, career concerns and so on. But Twitter rewards first acknowledgement of error, imperfection, and, in general, the "I didn't think of that, thanks" mentality. This is so refreshing.

Julio writes about the Twitter "fail whale," the icon associated with Twitter being out of service, and the subsequent way users have embraced the company's growing pains, with many trying to help Twitter improve.

That's what business needs to understand, that if there is mutual respect among Twitter users, there is mutual benefit. In such a situation, a company will be given the benefit of the doubt when mistakes occur, and will even get ideas from the Twitter community on how to improve. This concept has some of its roots in the wisdom of crowds. No single man, beast, or institution can have all the answers, but together we can do better.

Twitter Taps Human Need

Twitter is popular because it taps human needs—the desire we have as part of humanity to connect, to be curious, to seek recognition, to be part of something, and to share. This is heady stuff for most businesses to grasp, especially if they are accustomed to sending out direct mail, blasting television ads about the Labor Day Weekend sale, or requiring another 50 leads to make a quota.

As I reflect on Twitter and social media, I'm reminded of a Buffalo Springfield song: "There's something happenin' here... what it is ain't exactly clear." The beauty of Twitter is that it captures so much of the human experience while resisting any effort to compartmentalize it.

I'm glad that Julio wrote this book, and happy to see that he has a website dedicated to covering future aspects and details about Twitter. What is certain about today's social media is there always will be an afterward.

Albert Maruggi is a senior fellow at the Society for New Communications Research, and the president of the St. Paul-based Provident Partners public-relations and social-media agency. He has hosted the popular "Marketing Edge" podcast since early 2005; find it on Apple's iTunes Store.

About the Author

Julio Ojeda-Zapata has been on the front lines of the internet and computer revolutions as a syndicated columnist, editor and award-winning writer for more than a decade. He's an internet addict with a bulging RSS newsreader and thousands of tweets (he is at @jojeda and @twitinbiz). He writes for the St. Paul Pioneer Press, part of MediaNews Group. He lives in St. Paul, Minnesota, with his wife, son and a guinea pig called Pepita. Reach him at julio@twitin.biz.

Create Thought Leadership for your Company

Books deliver instant credibility to the author. Having an MBA or Ph.D. is great; however, putting the word "author" in front of your name is similar to using the letters Ph.D. or MBA. You are no long Michael Green, you are "Author Michael Green."

Books give you a platform to stand on. They help you to:

- Demonstrate your thought leadership
- Generate leads

Books deliver increased revenue, particularly indirect revenue:

- A typical consultant will make 3x in indirect revenue for every dollar they make on book sales

Books are better than a business card. They are:

- More powerful than white papers
- An item that makes it to the book shelf vs. the circular file
- The best tschocke you can give at a conference

Why Wait to Write Your Book?

Check out other companies that have built credibility by writing and publishing a book through Happy About.

Contact Happy About at 408-257-3000 or go to http://happyabout.info.

Other Happy About® Books

Purchase these books at Happy About
http://happyabout.info
or at other online and physical bookstores.

I'm on Facebook—Now What???

This book shows you how to get Business and Professional Value from Facebook

Paperback $19.95
eBook $11.95

Networking Online- Making LinkedIn Work for you!

This book explains the benefits of using LinkedIn and recommends best practices so that you can get the most out of it.

Paperback: $19.95
eBook: $11.95

The Emergence of The Relationship Economy

This book analyzes the factors that are influencing an emerging economy based on the sum of factors driving massive and significant changes to the way everyone will work, play, and live.

Paperback $21.95
eBook $14.95

Happy About Customer Service?

This book will develop your customer service standards so that you consistently, and to the endless pleasure of your customers, will deliver Customer Service Excellence.

Paperback $19.95
eBook $11.95

Additional Praise for this book

"Of all the up and coming technology and communication tools on the web, Twitter has mystified and empowered more people than any similar service. In 'Twitter Means Business,' Julio makes short work of demystifying Twitter, both on threats and opportunities for business. He provides an engaging mix of big-brand and small-business case studies, applications for PR, and a plethora of Twitter crowdsourced tips from—where else?—Twitter. This book is an excellent primer for companies and business professionals that want to really understand the impact of Twitter for business."
Lee Odden (@leeodden), CEO, TopRank Online Marketing

"In 'Twitter Means Business,' Julio profiles two of my Twitter friends, Comcast and JetBlue. Yes, these companies are now my friends because we talk, on Twitter. Thinking about using Twitter to connect with your customers and prospects? Julio provides case studies to guide you. Really, really great stuff."
Steve Garfield (@stevegarfield), pioneering video blogger and Boston Media Makers founder

"With 'Twitter Means Business,' Julio delivered a comprehensive guide for companies of any size to embrace microblogging. The many real examples and actionable tips point the reader to find and join the conversation. With this book, you are on you way to start a successful social-media program for your small business or global brand."
Julio Fernández (@SocialJulio), global-search and social-media strategist, GlobalStrategies.com

"This book captures Twitter's essence and explains its powerful ability of allowing businesses to converse with their customers."
Connie Bensen (@cbensen), online-community strategist, conniebensen.com

"Consider 'Twitter Means Business' required reading for those who believe Twitter's sole purpose is to give the self-absorbed an avenue to crack wise in 140 characters or less. Julio clearly spells out the practical purposes of Twitter for individuals and industry."
Christopher Breen (@BodyofBreen and @HairofBreen), Macworld Senior Editor and technology-book author

9 781600 051180